ADVENTURES OF A
DEAF-MUTE

GALLAUDET CLASSICS IN DEAF STUDIES

A SERIES EDITED BY

Kristen C. Harmon

ADVENTURES OF A DEAF-MUTE

and Other Short Pieces

William B. Swett

INTRODUCTION BY
Kristen C. Harmon

Gallaudet University Press
WASHINGTON, DC

GALLAUDET CLASSICS IN DEAF STUDIES

A SERIES EDITED BY
Kristen C. Harmon

Gallaudet University Press
Washington, DC 20002
http://gupress.gallaudet.edu

Library of Congress Cataloging-in-Publication Data

Names: Swett, William B., 1824-1884.
Title: Adventures of a deaf-mute, and other short pieces / William B. Swett ;
introduction by Kristen C. Harmon.
Description: Washington, DC : Gallaudet University Press, 2017. |
Series: Gallaudet classics in Deaf studies
Identifiers: LCCN 2016046696| ISBN 9781563686832 (pbk.) |
ISBN 9781563686849 (e-book)
Subjects: LCSH: Swett, William B., 1824-1884. |
Deaf—United States—Biography. | White Mountains (N.H. and Me.)—
Description and travel. | Hiking—White Mountains (N.H. and Me.) |
Sign language. | Finger spelling. | Gallaudet, T. H. (Thomas Hopkins),
1787–1851. | Clerc, Laurent, 1785-1869.
Classification: LCC HV2534.S94 S94 2017 |
DDC 362.4/1092 [B]—dc23
LC record available at https://lccn.loc.gov/2016046696

Cover photograph: *Old Man of the Mountain, Franconia Notch,
White Mountains* (between 1890 and 1901), from the Detroit Publishing
Company Photograph Collection in the Library of Congress Prints and
Photographs Division.

Images of William B. Swett, Thomas Hopkins Gallaudet,
and Laurent Clerc courtesy of Gallaudet University Archives.

Photograph of the Old Man of the Mountain at Night
Courtesy of the New York Public Library.

Contents

Introduction
Kristen C. Harmon

I always had a love of adventure, but made it a rule "never to get into danger until I had planned how to get out of it."
—William B. Swett

EACH SUMMER in the three years immediately following the end of the American Civil War, Deaf New Englander William B. Swett (1824–1884) worked as a carpenter, handyman, and guide for the famed Profile House, a hotel and tourist destination in the Franconia Range of the White Mountains of New Hampshire. The hotel took its name from a craggy collection of rocks on top of Cannon Mountain that resembled the profile of an old man, and this iconic image, known as "the old man of the mountains," adorns the New Hampshire quarter and postage stamps. Swett's many travails and adventures during those three summers working at Profile House formed the basis for *Adventures of a Deaf-Mute in the White Mountains,* a short memoir published and reprinted in 1869, 1874, and 1875.

Just about to turn forty years old that first summer in 1865, Swett began his adventures in the White Mountains under a dark cloud—two of his five children had died of diphtheria the year before, and, as a carpenter, he said the competition was "so great, I being a mute, I found it hard work to support a family" (75).[1] Additionally, in the years prior to the Civil War, he had been much "hindered in all kinds of work by sickness, and the expense more than [he] could get by steady work" (75). And so, reeling from the tragedies and setbacks of the years leading up to and during the Civil War, when Swett saw the advertisement for a "large gang of workmen" for the Profile House, he noted, "I may as well say here, that, while the wages offered were very acceptable, they had not so much to do with my decision as had a desire to see a place of which I had heard so much, and an idea that there would be some chance to gratify my love of adventure" (3).

"Of adventure," Swett went on to say, "I subsequently had a good deal" (3). His short but memorable account narrated in first person reads as a Deaf-centered accounting of adventures "abroad," in the company of hearing and nonsigning people. His travelogue does not begin with the leave-taking of his Deaf spouse, Margaret Harrington Swett (1826–1907), and it does not address or portray his life as a signing Deaf person from a multigenerational Deaf family from New Hampshire; it begins instead on the train platform in Concord, NH. In keeping with the title, *Adventures* begins with Swett's first step outward into this journey as the self-proclaimed "Deaf-Mute" of the title.*

With a great deal of self-possession and wry humor, Swett records the varied perceptions of deafness that he encounters; initial negative reactions, are, of course, more often converted into acceptance or outright admiration for Swett's abilities and skills. Confident in his identity as a Deaf "mute" (a non-speaking person) in this era, Swett's descriptions of his encounters often contain amusing observations of how the *other* portion of society perceives differences. While he feels compelled to counter negative stereotypes through demonstrations of his own able-bodiedness and cleverness, he does not feel the need to justify his own existence or explain or apologize for his Deaf signing identity. On that first journey up to the

---

* The term *deaf-mute* was commonly used by both deaf and hearing people in the time Swett was writing.

White Mountains, for example, Swett and his fellow travelers are caught in a snowstorm; having perched, by choice, on top of the stagecoach, Swett is especially relieved to see the "fire and hot supper" provided for them at the Profile House. Upon entering the hotel, Swett notes that

> my signs and gestures, and my little slate, of which I made free use in talking with my companions, soon attracted the attention of the company, to most of whom a deaf-mute was evidently a new thing. One man in particular, an Irishman, who was seated in a corner smoking a pipe, after eyeing me intently for some time, approached me, laid a hand on my shoulder, looked me in the face, and then, making the sign of the cross, he nodded, went back to his seat, and resumed his pipe, apparently satisfied that it was all right. I could not help smiling at his behavior, and did not know what to think of it; but have since concluded that it was his way of either getting acquainted or of expressing sympathy. (6–7)

This is not the last time Swett will encounter superstitious perceptions or, upon first meeting him, outright rejection. In one memorable instance, a man from New Jersey is told to hire Swett as a guide, but this man, Swett says, upon "learning that I was deaf and dumb . . . flatly refused to take me, adding some very uncomplimentary remarks, which were reported to me, of which I took no apparent notice, although I made a memorandum of them in my mind" (31). The man sets off alone up the mountain, becomes lost, and then, when Swett decides to search for him, is certainly very happy to see Swett. Swett leads him back down the mountain at a very quick pace (it was becoming dark), and Swett confesses to "having experienced a sort of malicious pleasure in leading him such a race, in consideration of his remarks on me the other day" (32). But true to Swett's good nature and generosity, he soon has the "pleasure" of seeing the man reunited with his anxious wife. For the remainder of his stay, the man from New Jersey hired Swett as his guide and said he'd never had a better guide in all his worldly travels.

Innovative, energetic, and full of fun and daring, Swett is an appealing guide to life in the postbellum era, a time when major cities were finally linked by railroad, the cost of transportation dropped, and tourism soared.[2] In short sketches describing his experiences and various events during the tourist season of the years from 1865 to 1867, Swett recounts the many hair-raising escapades he undertakes and survives.

At the end of his first summer at the Profile House, just because he could, Swett decided late one afternoon to hike up to the very top of the head of the "Old Man," plant a pole and flag there, and then build a bonfire that could be seen below. This was an arduous climb that few had made. He succeeds, but nearly slips to his death and almost gets caught out overnight without a lantern and provisions. While up on the mountain, cold and wet through with perspiration, Swett remembers the story of Charles Barrett, a "wealthy deaf-mute of Boston, now dead" (16), who had visited the mountain in 1859 as part of a group attending a convention in Vermont. Barrett was unprepared, became lost, and suffered what was most certainly hypothermia. Swett, however, knows the mountain and rests in a cleft in a rock, away from wind, until it is time to light the fire, which is seen by the three hundred and fifty guests of the hotel. Afterward, he slowly, but surely, makes his way down the mountain at night, without a lantern.

When the hotel guests take up a collection of money for him, Swett thanks them, but then says he could not be paid to undertake the same ordeal again: a "man will sometimes do a thing for his own gratification which he cannot afterward be hired to do at any price" (18). However, the very next day, Swett sees that he planted the flagpole not on the head of the profile but instead on the "Adam's Apple," a collection of rocks nearby. "Not content to leave the job half done" (18), he rows across the lake once again, climbs up the mountain, and moves the pole, this time, to the right place.

Swett outwits Mother Nature and prolongs his "inevitable end" several times in narrow escapes from death or serious injury. He dodges under rock shelves and into small caves in torrential rain, and he dashes down away from the insidious, drifting "frost-clouds" and "frost demons" that could be and were deadly for those unprepared souls caught out in the elements and exposed even at the peak of summer.

He also engages in activities to entertain and assist the hotel guests. He takes it upon himself to build an outsized model of a panther out of painted wood and then carries it up the mountain himself, piece by large piece. The following summer, he builds and then sets an "Indian with a gun" on top of a distinctive outcropping of rocks, posed in the act of shooting the panther. Both summers, the hotel guests rewarded Swett with a "handsome purse." He coordinates what seems to be a lovely midsummer night's dream experience—hotel guests rowed out one night to the middle of Profile Lake to watch fireworks and a bonfire in a dark, starless night. He escorts a photographer—a veteran who had been half-blinded by flying shrapnel in a Civil War battle—to the famed scenic vistas of the Franconia Ridge. Both guide and photographer must haul packs each weighing 100 pounds and must cope with the mishaps that come along with hauling such heavy equipment over rugged terrain. These and other adventures are given to us in short, energetic, episodes.

In all of his adventures, Swett describes and counters negative stereotypes with a great deal of generosity and humor. It is refreshing to read such brisk and confident prose about navigating nonsigning spaces. He takes great pride in his physicality, stamina, and long legs, noting how the length of his legs comes in handy when trying to leap from one side of a deep, treacherous chasm to another.

Yet, a consistent sense of something just under the surface, an awareness of the fragility and limits of human bodies and the precariousness of life, comes up occasionally and then more overtly at the end when Swett is on his way home. In an incident that he says he will never forget, he sees a young girl in a chair peddling white birch baskets filled with blackberries to stagecoach passengers. When the bar controlling the horses' harnesses knocks her over, Swett sees that she has one leg. She loses all of the berries she intends to sell, but the passengers promptly jump out, raise her up, kiss her, and lift her back into her chair. Swett reports "her hands were soon well-filled with money," yet he never learns "how she came to lose her leg" (67). Even so, after this momentary pause, he makes his way home, "gratified with my THREE SUMMERS' ADVENTURES" (67; emphasis in original). After a detailed description of the landscape he sees on his way out of the White Mountains, including the infamous and tragic Willey House,[3] the adventures close there, with a final observation of the "various forms in which human nature crops out" (4).

Throughout this memoir, Swett returns, in subtle ways, to the idea that being "king of the mountain" is a fragile thing. When he reaches the peak of Cannon Mountain, he takes in the view and feels "for the time, 'monarch of all I surveyed'; but if my realm was limited by my vision, it was small indeed, and my crown by no means sat lightly on my brow" (17). Cannon Mountain, and its rocky outcropping in the shape of an old man's profile, holds a special fascination for Swett.

> To the general observer, who sees the "Old Man" against a clear sky, the expression is one of earnest expectation, mingled with that "heart-sickness produced by hope long deferred." But the expression varies with the weather. Sometimes it appears on the point

of giving utterance to speech; sometimes it wears a settled scowl, and at others a look of more than mortal sadness. (8)

In this revealing description of the "Old Man," Swett seems to be alluding to Proverbs 13:12—"Hope deferred makes the heart sick: but when the desire cometh, it is a tree of life." However, the "heart-sickness" alluded to here could also refer to a line from a gothic romance published in 1872, Mrs. Alexander Orr's *Flower of the Ticino*. A very close variation of this line comes up in the romance when a mother, waiting for months for news of her son, decides to set out to search for him. There is no evidence available that determines whether or not Swett read the Orr book; however, he writes, "look through nature up to nature's God" (21), which is almost identical to a line from "Luther: A Poem" by English poet Robert Montgomery (1807–1855). This poem, musing upon theologian Martin Luther's marriage and relationship to God and Nature, contains observations like the following:

Expressive mountains! from whose massive forms
The dread Almighty speaks Himself to man
. . . .
A mute theology all nature makes;
The very ground no vain religion breathes,
. . . .
Behold a centre where our Yearnings meet,
That oneness where all aspirations blend—
When o'er the ruins of Ourselves we roam;
And not from nature *up* to nature's God,
But *down* from nature's God, look nature through.[4]

While not overtly expressed as a goal of this set of adventures, Swett clearly is observing and taking in the beauty and dangers of the landscape and what it might mean for himself, a grieving father. Swett viewed and interpreted his experiences through a Christian or meditative lens, and the conclusions that he reaches are not clichéd, nor are they platitudes. If anything, his observations are open-ended, a series of linked associations and experiences rather than conclusions.

Written from the vantage point of someone who was no longer a young man but still very much in the prime of his life, Swett's series of adventure tales can be read as an energetic engagement with life and with the landscape; but read another way, these tales could also be seen as Swett's reflections after the deaths of his children. These are the stories of someone testing his physical and emotional limits. At one point, Swett ventures high up, on purpose, into a "frost-cloud" on the mountain because, as he says, "I wanted to *feel* how cold it was, and to ascertain how far I could endure it" (29). Swett does not have adventures for the sake of adventure; instead, his adventures are, perhaps, a reflection on how to live a mortal, finite, life surrounded by compatriots or surrounded by strangers. Shortly after arriving at Profile House, Swett ponders the landscape.

> I spent the rest of the day in looking out of the windows upon the grand scenery with which it is surrounded, and in recalling to mind the mountain adventures and narrow escapes of which I had read, and trying to remember how the persons concerned acted, in order to escape the danger they were in.
>
> I always had a love of adventure, but made it a rule "never to get into danger until I had planned how to get out of it"; and I think it very important and useful for people to study and remember *how to act* in case of exposure to any kind of danger. . . . A person with presence of mind has an immense advantage in case of accidents, . . . Knowledge how to act has saved my own life and limbs several times. (8–9)

Testing the limits, facing and overcoming danger due to knowing how to act: these are Swett's paramount concerns. But his stories are also the tales of someone who finds plenty to do with his hands and tools to "keep off any sense of loneliness" (62).

In the *Adventures,* time moves in geological cycles; in the smallness of a particular moment, humans share the space with the prey and predators of the landscape. On Eagle Cliff, Swett watches a rabbit pop in and out of his burrow in an attempt to evade an eagle; the eagle fails at first and soars aloft again. Swett has a "momentary wish for a gun," but the next minute he is ashamed of himself, "for it seemed almost a crime to shoot such a bird." Then, the eagle swoops back down and catches the "unlucky rabbit in its claws, sail[s] gracefully away over the forest, and disappear[s] behind the cliff" (22). Before Swett leaves that spot on Eagle Cliff, he notices a huge slab, seemingly perched on the edge of the cliff, ready to slide down. The next spring, the boulder does indeed slide, and he watches it crash and "tear" down the side of the mountain. The next morning, he joins a party to see the aftermath.

> The immense mass of rock had cleared a path for itself for many rods below, sweeping the trees before it like chaff, and grinding some of them to powder. Rocks, large and small, were scattered far and wide, as they had been hurled from the path of the slab. . . . I am inclined to think a number of such slides, at different periods, are what caused the outline of a human face known as "The Old Man," and I also think that, in time, other slides will occur which will entirely obliterate it." (23)

And indeed, in 2003, the distinctive outcropping of rocks forming the profile of "The Old Man" collapsed.

Swett's fascination with the "Old Man" continued throughout his time at the Profile House. He wrote that he would often hit his own fingers while hammering because he had been gazing up at the mountain and the changeable expressions there. The second summer, Swett decided to make a "fac-simile" of the profile in calcined plaster (plaster of Paris). Using large sheets of cotton cloth and a clothesline, Swett "risk[s] my wife's husband's neck" (38) on the rocks to take the measure of the rocks forming the profile. He then uses the measurements to make a copy of the profile true to the proportions and form of the original. So successful was Swett's model that he was written up in the *New York Journal of Commerce* and on September 30, 1866, the *New York Times* reprinted a short article entitled, "The 'Old Man of the Mountain,'— A Daring and Ingenious Deaf Mute."

The hazardous adventures recounted here were originally published as individual sketches in *Deaf-Mutes' Friend*, the monthly journal that Swett published with Deaf writer, journalist, and editor William M. Chamberlain. The *Deaf-Mutes' Friend*, which ran only for one year, in 1869, was one of the earliest community-oriented Deaf newspapers. It was one of several publications that came out to supplement the *American Annals of the Deaf*, which focused largely on education and to which both hearing and deaf writers contributed.[5] In the salutatory in the first issue of *Deaf-Mutes' Friend*, Chamberlain wrote,

> For over a year we have been receiving letters from mutes and their friends in all parts of the country, saying that a paper was greatly needed which should be devoted to the true interests of the deaf and dumb and an organ of communication between the widely scattered thousands who once shared the same games and studies at the various Institutions for their class which exist in nearly every State in the Union, thereby keeping alive the friendships of former years and giving information of the welfare of each and all.[6]

Intending to "promise our readers some months of entertainment from the material," Swett published his initial accounts of life in the White Mountains in monthly installments throughout 1869, following a chronological sequence of events.[7] Chamberlain, in the editorial notes for the very first issue of *Deaf-Mutes' Friend*, explained that the sketches had been compiled from both Swett's written notes as well as translations from Swett's signed narratives: "Mr. Swett . . . gives much of the material in the colloquial 'language of signs,' the expressive and comprehensive language of the deaf-mutes, and we are obliged to translate it into English. How well or ill this is done, is not for us to say."[8] The serial publication of the *Adventures*, along with how the sketches were compiled, likely resulted in the short, episodic, action-oriented, structure of the narratives themselves.

After serialization and the end of *Deaf-Mutes' Friend*, Swett's adventures were expanded and reprinted as an entire collection in 1874 and again in 1875. Proceeds from the 1874 print run went to benefit the Boston Deaf-Mutes' Mission and the Boston Deaf-Mutes' Library Association; the profits from the sale of some 15,000 copies led to a reprint in 1875, this time benefiting Swett himself. The writer of the introduction of the 1875 edition says that Swett "has been taken ill, and disabled entirely from any work whatever, besides losing the sight of one eye and being uncertain of saving the other." There is no mention of DeafBlindness in the adventures recounted here, and it is unclear whether or not Swett ever self-identified as a DeafBlind person. However, Swett's Deaf grandfather, Nahum Brown, was described as having suffered from "severe headaches" late in life, becoming blind in one eye and then in the second.[9]

Born into a multigenerational Deaf family in Henniker, New Hampshire, in 1824, William B. Swett is believed to have been hard of hearing early on and then lost the remainder of his hearing due to the measles and mumps at ten years of age. His grandfather Nahum Brown (1772–1859) was the first deaf person in the family. Brown had two deaf children, Persis (1800–1869), who was Swett's mother, and Thomas (1804–1886). Thomas Brown was a founding member and president of the New England Gallaudet Association of Deaf Mutes, a man described as "the first great American Deaf leader."[10] Upon graduation from the American Asylum for the Deaf in Hartford, Connecticut, in 1842, Swett married Margaret Harrington, an Irish Deaf woman and a graduate of the New York School for the Deaf.[11] The Brown and Swett families were key members of the Henniker, New Hampshire, Deaf community, one of three significant New England Deaf communities that flourished and became the "roots" of the contemporary "Deaf-World" in the United States.[12]

Alexander Graham Bell included a detailed analysis of the Swett and Brown families in his discussion of possible genetic patterns of inheritance of deafness among Deaf families in "Memoir Upon the Formation of a Deaf Variety of the Human Race" (1884).[13] Indeed, a list of the Swett and Brown families and friends at such events as the 1850 "Grand Reunion" of American Asylum alumni reads like a "who's who" of the early New England Deaf communities that grew in and around the American Asylum in the mid-nineteenth century. Swett and his wife, Margaret Harrington Swett, were in attendance at the 1850 event, the "first major public event sponsored by and for Deaf people."[14]

In the years before and after he headed to the White Mountains, Swett had "a colorful career as an explorer, showman, mechanic, writer, and artist."[15] "Imbued with the spirit of adventure," he at one point in his life reportedly "embarked upon a whaling voyage to the frozen wilds of the North, from which he gleaned a vast fund of information that he was always delighted to bestow upon others."[16]

"Born to be an inventor," Swett "invented several things, such as doctor's pocket scales [sic], a key and lock, an artificial water-fall," and so on (74, 77). While a student at the American Asylum, Swett became fascinated with a diorama of the Battle of Bunker Hill that he had seen on display in Hartford's City Hall.[17] Dioramas were painted, moving, three-dimensional miniatures that depicted scenes of important events, usually battles. The more well-known dioramas, such as Lewis and Bartholomew's Battle of Bunker Hill, were not "'a mere painting'; the medium was 'a combination of mechanism and scenery,' having some chemical, color and lighting effects, with simulated war din and musical accompaniments. It contained 'all kinds of properties and representation of human beings,' that 'added verisimilitude' and increased the illusion of reality." Miniature figures were dressed and posed as soldiers, with movable joints. As "mechanical theater," the Lewis and Bartholomew diorama that Swett witnessed at the Hartford City Hall enacted the Battle of Bunker Hill in three acts.[18]

Swett never forgot the experience of seeing Lewis and Bartholomew's Battle of Bunker Hill. Years later, he told a group of students, "Time never can erase it out of my mind, on seeing the first scene, how I was startled and enraptured, and would not turn away my eyes from the moving figures, and I wondered if they had souls, until the performance was through" (see p. 73, this volume). So taken was he by the diorama that he devoted years to learning how to whittle and design the figures and pieces of a military scene, and he created a diorama of the Battle of Lexington. As he said later, "I learned two words, patience and perseverance. When I lay hold of any thing, I go to work with a will and overcome all difficulties if I meet them" (74). Indeed, after his death, Swett was described by his compatriots as having been "gifted to a remarkable degree with courage and perseverance, no sooner did one trade fail him than he immediately applied himself to another. . . . He mastered thoroughly whatever he undertook, and invariably won the respect of his associates by his quiet demeanor and upright dealings."[19]

In 1858, a Manchester (NH) newspaper reported that "Mr. Wm. B. Swett, of this town, a deaf-mute has recently given an exhibition here which will illustrate the skill and ingenuity as well as the indomitable patience and perseverance of the Yankee character." Swett's Battle of Lexington consisted of 300 figures moved by "hidden machinery, re-enacting the battle." The article noted that after six years of construction of the diorama, Swett hoped to raise the funds to perfect and present the work to the larger public.[20]

On Christmas Day of 1858, Swett exhibited the Battle of Lexington to students at the American Asylum in Hartford and gave a short address. A charming reflection on childhood, creativity, and perseverance in the face of naysayers and the challenges of adult life, "Mr. Swett and His Diorama" provides insight into Swett's life and history before embarking on his journey to the White Mountains (see pp. 69–78, this volume).

After the cheerful, breezy adventure stories and "tales of derring-do" of the *Adventures*, readers may be struck by the difference in tone and the much more vulnerable and revealing content in his address to the students at the Hartford school. While Swett portrayed confidence and cultivated a somewhat distanced and objective narration towards his hearing compatriots in *Adventures*, his address at the Hartford school is much more reflective and intimate. For one, his memories of being a student at the school come flooding back for him; he confesses that "I am totally incapable of saying what the expressions of my heart are while I stand before you" (72). He discusses some of the challenges of his life after graduation, including the difficulty in finding steady work in his trade. Swett makes special mention of his wife Margaret, telling the students,

All the success I met with [on the diorama] is owing much to my wife's encouragement and kind advice. She would lessen or drive away any gloomy thoughts that I was always apt to bear, and she would bear all the troubles with me with great patience, and I confess I have been more than once morose and cross to her in the day of trouble, but thank her for her kind look. When I succeeded, after a long time, in finding out a method I could work the figures, how her eyes brightened up! . . . and she often and alone of all my friends urged me along, showing pictures of future happiness and comfort to us all, put to silence so much malicious stories against us. (76)

Swett and his wife had five children (three hearing, two deaf), but two died in 1864, shortly before the opening of Swett's *Adventures*. Said to have been "deeply depressed" by the loss of his children, James and Addie, Swett then left to become a handyman and guide in the White Mountains.[21] In the years after he returned home, he became involved in Deaf social organizations along with his uncle Thomas Brown. He published with Chamberlain the monthly paper, *Deaf-Mutes' Friend*, became director of the Deaf-Mute Library Association, served as business manager for the Boston Deaf-Mute Mission, and was the first secretary of the New England Gallaudet Association and, later, its president.[22]

In addition to *Adventures of a Deaf-Mute*, Swett published *Manual Alphabets and their History, with Sketches, Illustrations, and Varieties*, in 1875 (see pp. 79–93, this volume). An overview of the one-handed and two-handed manual alphabets, this booklet also included short biographies of Thomas Hopkins Gallaudet and Laurent Clerc. Proceeds from this publication were intended to "derive sufficient profit to support [Swett's] family, he being now disabled from any work, with poor bodily health, and a disease of the eyes which has destroyed one and threatens the other."[23]

Despite his ill health, Swett went on to found the New England Industrial School for the Education and Instruction of Deaf-Mutes in Beverly, MA, in 1879. He served as superintendent, his wife served as matron, and their daughters, Ellen ("Nellie") and Lucy, were teachers. Upon Swett's death in 1884, Rev. Thomas Gallaudet wrote that "the kind-hearted, skillful workman has been called to his rest in Paradise, but the work he began will go on."[24] In other remarks after Swett's death, his compatriots noted that

> To [the object of establishing the New England Industrial School], he devoted his untiring energies for five years, and the results have excited the admiration of the public. He had effected vast improvements upon the building and grounds, doubling their value. The only thing wanting to complete his joy was the recognition of the State Board of Education. Just as the State Board was proceeding to act favorably on the petition of the Trustees of the School, Mr. Swett was cut off in his prime by the remorseless and inexorable hand of death. . . . but his work may yet live after him, and stand as a useful, beneficent monument to his memory."[25]

At Swett's memorial service in Beverly, MA, the pupils of the school, "twenty in number, arose to take the last look at the face of their friend and benefactor, there was evidence of the love which they bore for him who was no more. One little fellow, sobbing bitterly, could, with difficulty, be induced to leave his seat and walk past the coffin."[26] Swett was said to be "always careful of giving offence, saying very little himself and keeping his temper under perfect control, no man ever lived who was so much respected as he was by the community among whom his lot was cast."[27] After her father's death just a few short years after the founding of the school, Ellen

Harrington Swett became superintendent, a position she retained for twenty years, until her death in 1904.[28] The school was renamed the Beverly School for the Deaf in 1922, and it is still in operation.

READERS OF *Adventures of a Deaf-Mute in the White Mountains* will be struck by the glimpses of postbellum American life; while the Civil War is barely mentioned, the aftermath of a divided United States at war emerges occasionally. Swett narrates an encounter he had with Admiral David Farragut, and he describes his own "hero-worship" and "Yankee-like response" to the Civil War naval hero. Swett is gratified when Farragut tells him that he was—as was Swett himself—"acquainted with the veteran Laurent Clerc, who came from France, the first instructor of deaf-mutes in America, and others of our notable men" (25). The vocabulary and rhetoric of a war-torn nation comes up in descriptions of a rock formation as a "grim sentinel" (19), and when Swett and his co-workers engage in a joyous and sustained snowball fight in the middle of summer, they use tactics that "would have been useful on a more earnest battle-field" (10–11). Swett never discusses the Civil War at length, probably because his intent with this collection was to provide entertainment and to provide tales of adventure.

After the Civil War, the cost of transportation declined and many more people traveled further afield, particularly to mountain and seaside resorts. The Profile House, built in 1853, drew the "well-to-do" tourists and was a palatial and grand destination. By 1860, approximately 10,000 visitors came to the White Mountains every summer, and the Profile House was a key destination, located as it was in the Franconia Notch.[29] Swett describes the visitors as being artists, ramblers, and seekers of scenic views and peace, who sought refuge from "the duties and cares of life in the outside world" (62), and he portrays the Profile House in glowing terms.

It has four hundred windows, and can accommodate several hundred guests. . . . It is one of the most convenient, commodious, and best-managed hotels in the Mountains; it is within easy distance of some of the most interesting of the natural curiosities: Eagle Cliff, Echo and Profile Lakes, the Cascade and Falls, the "Old Man," the Basin, Pool, and Flume, Walker's Falls, and other minor objects. With its telegraph and stage offices, its hosts of servants and hundreds of guests, it is a town in itself. . . . The stables are extensive, as the travel demands it, and I have often counted three hundred and fifty horses stabled at once. (20)

Architectural historians note the importance of the Profile House and other regional inns for the burgeoning hotel industry in the years after the railroad expanded.[30] Above the hotel, Swett writes, Eagle Cliff "towers far into the air, and seems almost to overhang the hotel, although it is in reality quite a distance off" (21). A "billhead" photograph from 1867 does indeed show a massive wooded cliff with, at its foot, a large white four-story structure with wings and many dormer peaks on its sloping roofs, people milling about outside, and a stagecoach and riders on horseback pulling up to the entrance.[31] This popular hotel continued to expand, advertising itself in 1864 as "the largest of the leading Summer Hotels with a patronage of the highest order." After multiple expansions, it burned down in 1923.[32]

During the tourist season of 1866, Swett was hired as a guide and assistant for an unnamed "seedy-looking" photographer from New York who had come to "take views of the places of interest in the Mountains" (26). Swett says he was "not a very prepossessing individual," but he "wore an army uniform, and had only one eye, black and piercing" (26), having lost sight in the other during the Civil War at the Battle of Malvern Hill. Swett later found out this photographer had been part of Dr. Elisha Kent Kane's expedition to the Arctic Circle and Baffin Bay to search for the missing British explorer Sir John Franklin. This man was very likely Amos Bonsall (1830–1915), a member of the second Grinnell Expedition of 1853–1855. As the photographer of the Kane mission, Bonsall has a place in both photographic and Arctic exploration history. Swett reports that the "intense cold prevented [the photographer] from taking views, and he was otherwise employed" in the Kane expedition (26). Bonsall had brought and used daguerreotype equipment, but "all images were lost on an ice floe."[33]

These daguerreotypes would have been among the very first photographic images of this frozen region of the world, and there is some mystery about what happened to them. Despite what Bonsall told Swett and the visitors of the Profile House, Dr. Isaac Israel Hayes, the surgeon on the expedition, reported in 1853 that Bonsall had taken "a number of fine pictures," overcoming difficulties in working with the photographic chemicals. Bonsall later wrote that on the voyage home, "[t]he box containing the daguerreotypes was put upon a sledge on the ice, and was carried away, together with the whole collection of Arctic birds, which had been prepared with great care for the Academy of Natural Science. This was an irreparable loss, and one to this day I have never ceased to regret."[34] Even so, daguerreotypes said to be from the Kane expedition were put on display in Philadelphia in 1876. Photographic historian Martha Sandweiss says that

> these accounts are hard to reconcile with Bonsall's claim that the daguerreotypes sank in the cold Arctic sea. But they begin to suggest something of the vagaries of the daguerrean marketplace and the ways in which the daguerreotypes came to be revalued once the technology that produced them became obsolete. As alternatives to field sketches, daguerreotypes might

have seemed inadequate. But as historical artifacts they could be valued, long after the fact."[35]

Kane and his crew members were later celebrated as among the early non-indigenous explorers of the Arctic Circle, and Bonsall continued to work as a photographer in the years afterward.

Bonsall's arrival at the Profile House in October of 1866 was untimely and beset with challenges related to the rugged terrain, the increasingly wintry weather, and the unwieldiness of the equipment. Both Bonsall and Swett carried 100-pound loads up and over the mountains as Swett guided Bonsall to various scenic views. Swett cleared paths for Bonsall, they had mishaps with the equipment, they were caught out overnight in the "gloom of the forest" and had to make do with moss and blankets and no fire, and they evaded an "almost certain death" from sudden and deadly "frost-clouds" (28, 29). The weather was so uncooperative that Bonsall gave up and bade farewell to the Mountains.

THROUGH HIS many adventures in and out of the White Mountains, Swett witnessed some of the major developments of the antebellum and postbellum era in America: the public commemorations of the Revolutionary War, the expansion of the country and the subsequent removal of indigenous populations, the extension of the railroad and travel into previously unlinked portions of the country, the rise of tourism, and the ongoing development of photographic methods. Swett also was a key participant and contributor to some of the important developments of the Deaf community in the nineteenth century. He was a member of two significant multigenerational Deaf families in New England, an early alumnus of the American Asylum in Hartford, CT, a writer and publisher of Deaf-centered works, a member of various Deaf civic organizations, and the founder of the New England Industrial School for Deaf-Mutes. With his roots in sign language, in early Deaf education, in early civic organizations for the Deaf community, Swett provides a unique insight into early Deaf America in New England. Perhaps his most memorable contribution, however, is in having shared, for a brief time, a life of adventure and the lesson to always have a plan for getting out of danger.

The frontispiece of *Adventures of a Deaf-Mute in the White Mountains* is a pen and ink portrait of a handsome man in his forties with dark, curly muttonchops. His dark hair is slicked straight back in the style of the time, and he is dressed in a crisp-looking white shirt, a bow tie, and a dark, tailored jacket. William B. Swett, adventurer, was a handsome man. But what is most striking about this portrait are the eyes; they look off into a far landscape. Swett has bags under his eyes, but his gaze is determined and focused, just as he was throughout his life.

Notes

1. Unless otherwise noted, numbers in parentheses following quotes refer to pages in this volume.
2. Weiss, "Tourism in America."
3. Ibid., 299. In 1826, a landslide killed all seven members of the Willey family along with two hired men, but their house was spared. The Willey House became a popular tourist destination in the years afterward. Swett refers to it as Wiley House.
4. Montgomery, *Luther: A Poem*, 221, 225–26.
5. Edwards, *Words Made Flesh*, 110.
6. Chamberlain and Swett, "Salutatory," 17.
7. Chamberlain, "Life and Adventures of William B. Swett," 2.
8. Ibid., 1.
9. H.W.S., introduction to *Adventures of a Deaf-Mute*, 3; Lane, Pillard, and French, "Origins of the Deaf World," 21.
10. Lane, Pillard, and French, "Origins of the Deaf World," 18, 20.
11. "Ingenious Mechanism," 118; Edwards, *Words Made Flesh*, 233; Lane, Pillard, and French, "Origins of the Deaf World," 29.
12. Lane, Pillard, and French, "Origins of the Deaf World," 17.
13. Bell, *Formation of a Deaf Variety of the Human Race*, 205.
14. Edwards, *Words Made Flesh*, 125–26.
15. Lane, Pillard, and French, "Origins of the Deaf World," 29.
16. White, "Late Wm. B. Swett," 14.
17. "Lewis, Bartholomew, & Co. Respectfully Announce Their Arrival in this City with their Magnificent Historical Moving Diorama," Connecticut Digital Archive, accessed May 18, 2016, http://collections.ctdigitalarchive.org/islandora/object/40002:20171.
18. Arrington, "Lewis and Bartholomew's Mechanical Panorama," 53, 54.
19. White, "Late Wm. B. Swett," 14.
20. "Ingenious Mechanism," 117–18.
21. Lane, Pillard, and French, "Origins of the Deaf World," 29, 33.
22. Edwards, *Words Made Flesh*, 233; Lane, Pillard, and French, "Origins of the Deaf World," 35.
23. Introduction to *Manual Alphabets* by Swett, 3.
24. "History," Beverly School for the Deaf, accessed August 9, 2016, http://cccbsd.org/about/history/; "New England Industrial School," 230–31.
25. White, "Late Wm. B. Swett," 15.
26. Ibid., 16.
27. Ibid., 14–15.
28. Sanders, "Ellen Harrington Swett," 225.
29. Weiss, "Tourism in America," 300, 306; Tolles, *Grand Resort Hotels*, 39.
30. Tolles, *Grand Resort Hotels*, 38.
31. "Billhead for the Profile House, Franconia Notch, New Hampshire, dated September 25, 1867," Historic New England, accessed May 20, 2016,

http://www.historicnewengland.org/collections-archives-exhibitions /collections-access/collection-object/capobject?gusn=GUSN-255052.
32. "Profile House and Cottages," 75; Tolles, *Grand Resort Hotels*, 39.
33. Hannavy, *Nineteenth-Century Photography*, 69.
34. Sandweiss, *Print the Legend*, 117; Bonsall, "After Fifty Years," 43.
35. Sandweiss, *Print the Legend*, 118.

Bibliography

Arrington, Joseph Earl. "Lewis and Bartholomew's Mechanical Panorama of the Battle of Bunker Hill." *Old-Time New England* (Fall-Winter 1951–1952): 50–58.

Bell, Alexander Graham. *Memoir Upon the Formation of a Deaf Variety of the Human Race*. Washington, DC: Government Printing Office, 1884.

Bonsall, Amos. "After Fifty Years." In *The White World: Life and Adventures Within the Arctic Circle Portrayed by Famous Living Explorers*, edited by Rudolf Kersting, 38–50. New York: Lewis, Scribner, and Co., 1902.

Chamberlain, W. M. "Life and Adventures of William B. Swett: Introductory, by the Editor." *Deaf-Mutes' Friend* 1, no. 1 (January 1869):1–2.

Chamberlain, W. M., and William B. Swett. "Salutatory." *Deaf-Mutes' Friend* 1, no. 1 (January 1869): 17.

Edwards, R. A. R. *Words Made Flesh: Nineteenth-Century Deaf Education and the Growth of Deaf Culture*. New York: New York University Press, 2012.

Hannavy, John, ed. *Encyclopedia of Nineteenth-Century Photography*. New York: Routledge, 2008.

"Ingenious Mechanism Constructed by a Deaf-Mute." *American Annals of the Deaf and Dumb* 10, no. 2 (1858): 117–18.

Lane, Harlan, Richard C. Pillard, and Mary French. "Origins of the Deaf World: Assimilating and Differentiating Societies and their Relation to Genetic Patterning." *Sign Language Studies* 1, no. 1 (2000): 17–44.

Montgomery, Robert. *Luther: A Poem*. 2nd ed. London: Francis Baisler/Hamilton, Adams, and Co./Tilt and Bogue, 1842. Accessed at Google Books May 19, 2016.

"Mr. Swett and His Diorama, Address by Mr. Swett." *American Annals of the Deaf and Dumb* 11, no. 1 (1859): 46–53.

"New England Industrial School." *American Annals of the Deaf and Dumb* 29, no. 3 (1884): 230–31.

New York Times. "The 'Old Man in the Mountain'—A Daring and Ingenious Deaf Mute." September 30, 1866.

"Profile House and Cottages." *Outlook: A Family Paper* 50 (July 14, 1894): 75.

Sanders, Lucy M. "Ellen Harrington Swett." *Association Review* 6 (1904): 224–26.

Sandweiss, Martha A. *Print the Legend: Photography and the American West.* New Haven, CT: Yale University Press, 2002.

Swett, William B. *Adventures of a Deaf-Mute.* Marblehead, MA: William B. Swett, 1875.

Tolles, Bryant F. *The Grand Resort Hotels of the White Mountains: A Vanishing Architectural Legacy.* Boston: David R. Godine, 1998.

Weiss, Thomas. "Tourism in America before World War II." *Journal of Economic History* 64, no. 2 (2004): 289–327.

White, Harry. "Funeral of the Late William B. Swett." *Fourth Annual Report of the New England Industrial School for the Education and Instruction of Deaf-Mutes,* 14–16. Beverly, MA: New England Industrial School, 1884.

ADVENTURES OF A
DEAF-MUTE

PART ONE

Adventures of a Deaf-Mute in the White Mountains

First Summer

How I Happened to Go to the Mountains

EARLY IN the year 1865, the proprietors of the Profile House, in the Franconia Mountains, finding repairs and additions necessary to their hotel, advertised for a large gang of workmen.

I received a pressing invitation to go up and work. The wages were good, and expenses paid both ways.

I hesitated—there was work enough at home; I had never been out of work a single day, having always been sought for to do all kinds of work both in and out of town. I was acknowledged to be a skillful and steady workman. I hesitated, also, because my family and myself had been thrown into deep mourning by the recent death, from diphtheria, of two of our children, our only boy and a girl; but after a few days of reflection and consultation with my family, I decided to go.

I may as well say here, that, while the wages offered were very acceptable, they had not so much to do with my decision as had a desire to see a place of which I had heard so much, and an idea that there would be some chance to gratify my love of adventure.

Of adventure I subsequently had a good deal, as will be shown in the course of my story.

I notified several persons, who were waiting for me to do some work for them, that they must find some one else to do it, as I must go. They told me that they would wait until my return; and, bidding my family good-by, I was whirled away over the iron track.

At Concord, N.H., while waiting for the train from Boston, I noticed a strange-looking old man in the depot. His hair and beard were long and white, giving him a very patriarchal look.

The day was very cold, but he wore a straw hat and thin summer clothes, and his neck and feet were bare. He walked about with great activity, taking snuff frequently from a bladder, which served him instead of a box. He looked sharply at everyone, and spoke to me once; but when I put a finger to my ear and shook my head, he walked away. I wondered who and what he was, and inclined to think him either insane or very odd. I have since seen him going about the streets of Concord barefooted, and dressed in thin clothes, when the snow lay a foot deep on the ground.

His name is Flagg; he lives in a log cabin at Pembroke, about fifteen miles from Concord. He professes to be a water-cure doctor, and is about seventy-five years old.

Speculation in the various forms in which human nature crops out, helped me to pass away the time till the train came along.

Before reaching Lake Village, the train stopped at a small station for a supply of wood and water. Here a very ragged and dirty little boy annoyed the passengers by passing up and down in the cars. Meeting the conductor, a large and powerful man, he pushed past him and would have gone out, but the conductor seized him and actually threw him out of a window upon a wood-car that was slowly moving in an opposite direction. This little incident made every one roar with laughter. The boy was not hurt, though he was probably somewhat frightened.

After passing Lake Village, I caught my first glimpse of the peak of Mount Washington, the highest of all the White Mountains. Its summit was wrapped in snow, and its sublime appearance gave me much food for thought.

As we rode along, I caught occasional glimpses of sheets of water, and at last the broad and beautiful Lake Winnipiseogee lay before me. I no longer wondered at the name given it by the Indians, if, as some say, it means "The Smile of the Great Spirit." It has been called the "Loch Lomond" of America.

Loch Lomond is a lake in Scotland, famous for its beauty, but it is generally admitted, by those who have seen both, that Winnipiseogee is the most beautiful of the two.

The late Hon. Edward Everett, speaking of a visit to this lake, said: "I have been something of a traveller in our own country—though not so much as I could wish—and in Europe have seen all that is most attractive, from the Highlands of Scotland to the Golden Horn of Constantinople—from the summit of the Hartz Mountains to the Fountain of Vaucluse; but my eye has yet to rest on a lovelier scene than that which smiles around you as you sail from Weir's Landing to Centre Harbor."

At the Pemigewasset House, in Plymouth, where the train stopped for dinner, I met that prince of good fellows, Hiram Bell, Esq., the landlord of the hotel; formerly the well-known and popular landlord of the Profile House. It was to him that I was indebted for the invitation to go and work in the Mountains.

The deaf-mutes who composed the party which visited the Profile House and went up Mount Lafayette, in 1858, will remember Mr. Bell as a liberal-hearted man and a genial friend. I shall elsewhere give an account of the adventures of this party, in connection with my own.

As the train neared Well's River, I was standing at the car door, looking out, and saw one of the car wheels fly off and roll down the bank. The next instant there was a terrible jarring; the stove-pipe was shaken out, and the passengers were thrown into confusion. I could hardly keep my feet, and concluded that I should be killed.

Some one gave the signal to "brake up" by pulling the cord that ran through the train, and it was stopped without accident. After this we moved slowly to the next stopping-place, where the damaged car was removed and the train sped on.

In due time I reached Littleton, from which place are stages to all parts of the Mountains. I was so anxious to secure a seat on the top of the stage, that I climbed upon it first and gave orders about my baggage afterwards.

Our six stout horses carried us along at a good rate; on the way, I had a fine view of the Mountains. One of the passengers pointed out Mount Lafayette to me. The day was clear, and I could see that snow was falling on the mountain-top, while below it was the vast, black ravine in which I afterwards nearly lost my life, of which I tell in the proper place.

After passing Franconia, noted for its iron mine, and as being one of the coldest places in the country, we saw a snow-storm coming down upon us, and for a few moments it completely enveloped and blinded us; when it cleared away, Mount Lafayette looked more majestic than before, in its mantle of white.

All symptoms of life, except ourselves, soon disappeared, and for some miles the road was through a gloomy forest, and at the end of this we arrived at the Profile House.

Few of us having been prepared for the storm and cold, the fire and a hot supper were very welcome indeed.

My signs and gestures, and my little slate, of which I made free use in talking with my companions, soon attracted the attention of the company, to most of whom a deaf-mute was evidently a new thing. One man in particular, an Irishman, who was seated in a corner smoking a pipe, after eyeing me intently for some time, approached me, laid a hand on my shoulder, looked me in the face, and then, making the sign of the cross, he nodded, went back to his seat, and resumed his pipe, apparently satisfied that it was all right. I could not help smiling at his behavior, and did not know what to think of it; but have since concluded that it was his way of either getting acquainted or of expressing sympathy.

I retired to bed but could not sleep; my new situation and my own thoughts kept me awake. I could feel the house shake from the action of the wind, which was blowing hard, and, gathering extraordinary strength from compression in its passage through the Notch, struck with great force upon the hotel, which, although a very large building, shook like a person with the ague.

In the morning I was quite sick, having caught a bad cold in my ride from Littleton. After breakfast I felt better and took a walk; the mountains, trees, rocks, and everything were covered with ice—the effect of the frost-clouds during the night—and in the rays of the rising sun everything glittered and glowed with all the colors of the rainbow. It was a magnificent sight; I thought of the fairy scenes in the "Arabian Nights."

The scene increased in beauty as the sun rose higher, till the frostwork began to dissolve in the warmth, and in a short time everything had returned to its usual dark and somber hue.

My next thought was to visit the "Great Stone Face," "The Old Man of the Mountain."

"The Old Man of the Mountain"

I had heard much of this great natural curiosity; and had thought that there must be *some* resemblance to a human profile, but I was not prepared for the "accurate chiselling and astonishing sculpture" which now met my eyes.

The "Profile" has "a stern, projecting, massive brow, which looks as if it contained the thought and wisdom of centuries." The nose is "straight, and finely cut." The lips are thin, and slightly parted, as if about to speak. The chin is "well thrown forward, and shows the hard, obstinate character of the 'Old Man,' who has faced the storms of ages with such unmoving steadiness."

As I stood there and looked at the towering cliff on which the "Old Man" is situated, all my appreciation of the grand and sublime in nature was awakened; and, mingled with other thoughts came longings for a closer acquaintance with the "Old Man" and dreams of "doing and daring" in those wild regions as none had ever done before.

To the general observer, who sees the "Old Man" against a clear sky, the expression is one of earnest expectation, mingled with that "heart-sickness produced by hope long deferred." But the expression varies with the weather. Sometimes it appears on the point of giving utterance to speech; sometimes it wears a settled scowl, and at others a look of more than mortal sadness.

Clouds passing under the chin or above and around the forehead materially soften the expression, and, by bearding and wigging the face, make it very lifelike. The best time to see it is in the afternoon, when the sun is behind it. After a cold rain, I have seen the "Old Man's" face glisten beautifully, and wear a smiling look.

During the four seasons which I have spent at the "Profile House," I have studied the "Old Man" in all its aspects as seen from below. It had a fascination for me which drew me to it in storm and in calm, by day and by night, in season and out of season. It was a strange and unaccountable influence and an irresistible impulse.

Often as I have looked upon the "Old Man," both far and near, I am not satisfied; it still has the old attraction for me, and I hope to continue my researches in the vicinity.

Returning to the hotel, I spent the rest of the day in looking out of the windows upon the grand scenery with which it is surrounded, and in recalling to mind the mountain adventures and narrow escapes of which I had read, and trying to remember how the persons concerned acted, in order to escape the danger they were in.

I always had a love of adventure, but made it a rule "never to get into danger until I had planned how to get out of it"; and I think it very important and useful for people to study and remember *how to act* in case of exposure to any kind of danger. If this were more generally practised, there would be much less loss of life. A person with presence of mind has an immense advantage in case of accidents, and is worth a hundred who are wild and distracted. Knowledge how to act has saved my own life and limbs several times.

The next day I was able to go to work, and was much amused by the whisperings and pointings of my fellow-workmen. They regarded me, for some time, as a strange person, and seemed to be much afraid of my slate and pencil. One of them, who stood near me one day when I pulled out my slate for some purpose, ran away as fast as possible, showing fear on his face; but whether in fun or earnest I did not know, nor did I care, so long as there was nothing offensive in the manner. In course of time they got over this, and treated me as one of themselves.

The Bowling Alley at the foot of Cannon Mountain, so called, had been entirely destroyed, and we were ordered to rebuild it. It was destroyed in the following manner:

It snowed for half a day, then a cold rain followed, which froze solid; then fell a foot of snow, and the next day was so warm that the snow melted, and not being absorbed by the frozen ground, ran down the mountain into the valley. Gulches and ravines were quickly flooded; brooks became rivers, and cascades grew to cataracts. Behind the alley ran a small brook, which, overflowing its banks, undermined it and swept it away. The hotel grounds were flooded, all the cellars filled with water, and much damage was done. After finishing the alley, we were put to shingling the Profile House, the size of which may be imagined from its taking eight men twelve days to finish the front side only, and on that alone they used fifty thousand feet of shingles.

Snow-balling in June

One warm day in June, I made one of a party of eight persons which ascended Cannon Mountain in search of quartz crystals, the distance being about a mile and a half.

It was my first experience in climbing mountains, and I was soon very tired. The path had been damaged by the spring freshets, and the ascent, hard at any time, was then unusually so.

The day was fine, but just as we reached the top of the mountain we were enveloped in clouds, and could neither go for the crystals or enjoy the fine view which can be had in clear weather.

We were obliged cautiously to retrace our steps lest we should lose our way. I was much disappointed, but comforted myself by the reflection that I could come again.

As we were descending, we saw, a short distance to one side of the path, a patch of snow, about an acre in extent and a foot deep, so situated in a hollow that the sun never shone upon it. We left the path and went toward it: while looking around, some one proposed a little fun. With the feelings of younger days, the members of the party, whose ages ranged from thirty-five to sixty, divided into equal bodies and took up positions, the agreement being to pelt each other until one party should be driven from the snow.

The snow was soft, and easily worked, and the snow-balls flew fast and furious for more than an hour, when the party to which I belonged were driven from the field by a skilful movement of the other party, under the lead of an old gentleman of sixty, whose tactics would have been useful on a more earnest battle-field, and obliged to surrender. The severe exercise had stirred our blood and put us in good humor, doing much to compensate us for the loss of our original object in coming up the Mountain; and we resumed our homeward way, well pleased with the novel and uncommon incident of making and using snow-balls in summer.

At Work in the "Flume"

I went one day with a gang of workmen to repair the bridge over the Pemigewasset River, and the footways by which visitors reach the "Flume." The storms and freshets of winter always do more or less damage to the bridges, foot-paths, plank-walks, and other contrivances for the convenience, comfort and safety of the summer visitor, which are not removed at the close of the travelling season.

I will try to give those who have not seen it some idea of this great natural curiosity.

The "Flume" is reached from the bridge across the river, by a foot-path which follows the course of the stream, crossing it often, leading up and over steep rocks, and sometimes following the bed of the stream itself. At every step something is seen to admire.

The stream pours itself through the "Flume" over an inclined plane of smooth, polished rock, six hundred feet in length, and very gradual in descent. Precipices from sixty to eighty feet high wall in the waters on each side; the space between them averages about twenty feet, except at the upper end, where the walls suddenly approach each other within ten feet, and hold suspended between them, in mid-air, an enormous boulder of granite, which looks as if a very small force would send it into the stream below, so slight appears its hold between the cliffs. The precipices on each side are fringed with tall forest trees, and the sun shines into the ravine only about two hours a day. It is at all times a grand and gloomy scene.

The only way to get up this narrow gorge is by a foot-way of planks and logs which is kept in repair by the proprietors.

A huge tree has fallen across from one side to the other, above the boulder, and many persons have crossed the ravine on it. It is a dizzy height, and the foothold is not very secure, the log being rotten and slippery.

Having repaired the bridge, we proceeded to the "Flume" to fix up the foot-ways. We there found an army of small black flies, or midgets, as they are called. These troublesome little insects, which are far worse than mosquitoes, abound in the woods and all over the mountains, and annoy every one with merciless perseverance. They seldom show themselves in the houses, and will keep away from a person who is smoking. All workmen outside are obliged to make a fire and keep up a smoke, in order to be able to work. We built a huge fire at one end of the "Flume," and thus kept the flies away; a gust of wind would sometimes drive so much smoke in upon us as to compel us to drop our tools, and run out to avoid suffocation. This hindered us a good deal, but we preferred to be smoked out occasionally rather than to bear the constant torment of the flies.

The logs on which the plank foot-ways of the previous summer had rested having been washed away, it was necessary for us to cut down some trees for new ones; in order to procure what we needed, we ascended a narrow path to the top of one side of the ravine, and, cutting down the trees, we trimmed them and rolled them over the brink into the chasm below.

Looking over to the opposite side of the ravine, I saw a tall tree standing on the edge of the precipice, and determined to go across and fell it; I wished to see it fall into the "Flume" with all its branches on. Taking my axe, I started over the log I have spoken of as lying across the chasm; I had nearly reached the other side when my foot struck a projecting knot, I lost my balance, and what saved me from falling was a desperate spring, and my grasp on a bush which grew near the edge. I was startled, and it was some time before I could go to work; at last I began to cut down the tree, which soon began to reel, and the breeze taking it on the right side, it slowly inclined in the desired direction; I ran to a safe distance, and leaned over the edge as far as I dared, with one hand grasping the branch of a tree, to see it fall. It went down head-foremost, and was, to my surprise, considerably shorter than the depth of the ravine; it struck on its head, stood upright for an instant, as if surprised at its novel situation, and then its heavy butt-end went down on the bed of the stream with a crash like that of a thousand thunders. The earth shook and trembled beneath my feet, and the sensations I then experienced will never be forgotten.

I felled two more trees, but not with the same success, and, we having enough for the footways, I looked about for a way to the bottom of the ravine. The log by which I had crossed was still open to me, and a path was on the other side; but as I did not wish to trust the log again, I finally scrambled down the steep side of the precipice, and reached the bottom with only a few trifling bruises and scratches. We were obliged to work, much of the time, in three or four feet of water, which was cold as ice, and were very glad when the job was finished.

Almost an Accident

Early on the morning of the Fourth of July, the mulatto hostler of the Profile House brought a small cannon, or swivel, into the front yard. It had been used, the previous summer, for the entertainment of the guests who wished to hear the echoes waked by its discharge on the shore of Echo Lake, and had become rusty by long exposure to the weather. The mulatto filled the cannon nearly full of fine sporting gunpowder, grass and dirt, rammed it down as hard as possible, and then, lighting a match, attempted to discharge it; failing to do so, he gave it up for the present, and left the cannon in the yard. Another man came along, discovered how the cannon was loaded, and removed it to the back side of the hotel. Having reached a distance which he considered safe, he inserted a fuse in the priming, lit it, and ran away. The cannon burst; and a piece of iron weighing twenty pounds went over the Profile House and buried itself in the front yard, less than four feet from one of the guests who was walking there. It was very fortunate that the mulatto did not succeed in discharging the cannon; he would have been torn in pieces, and much other damage would have been done.

My First Visit to the "Old Man"

About the last of July I determined to pay a visit to the head of the "Old Man." While getting ready for the attempt, I thought, if I got there, I would set up a pole and raise a flag; I also concluded to remain on the top of the Mountain until after dark, and then build a large bonfire. I procured a hatchet, which I always thereafter carried in my belt in all my wanderings, a flag ten feet long and five feet wide, a long cord, a bag of shavings, and kindling-wood and some provisions; altogether they made a heavy load to carry to the top of the Mountain, a mile and a half, on a hot day in summer.

At one o'clock, P.M., I left the Profile House, and commenced the ascent of Cannon Mountain, so called from there being, near its top, a rock, which, seen from a certain point, resembles a cannon mounted on a carriage; it is also called Profile Mountain, as it is on its side that the "Old Man" is situated.

I followed the footpath, and found it very hard work to get along with my load, but reached the top, and deposited it in a convenient place for use at the proper time. After resting a little, I began to descend toward the "Old Man," which lies about a mile away in an opposite direction from that in which I ascended. The way was far more difficult than I had supposed; huge rocks were scattered around, among and over which I had to carefully choose my way. Long before I saw any signs of the "Old Man," I was much inclined to give it up; but I remembered that some one had been on the Head before, and that "what man has done, man may do."

I might not be, and probably was not, following the route taken by the other party, but any way to the Head must be hard and dangerous; so I pushed on, and was finally rewarded, as I supposed, by arriving at the spot I wished to find. Looking about for a flag-staff, I saw that the nearest wood was half a mile farther down, and that much of the way to it lay along the brink of a frightful precipice. The descent required great care; for in some places a slip of the foot would send me to be dashed in pieces on the rocks more than a thousand feet below, and a false step anywhere would be a serious thing. I finally reached the wood, and selected a fine stick, fifteen feet long, and five inches in diameter at the larger end, which I trimmed with my hatchet, and succeeded, after immense labor, in transporting to what seemed to be the right place. From the spot where I stood I could see the lake at the foot of the Mountain, and many people on the shore. I had told no one of my intentions when I left the hotel, and now began to regret it, as, if anything prevented me from getting back, nobody would know where to look for me, and the consequences might not be pleasant. However, by getting on a large rock and waving the flag, I attracted the attention of the people, who waved hats and handkerchiefs to show that they saw me. I now felt easier in my mind, as, if I was missed, my location would readily be inferred.

Raising the pole, I placed it in a cleft in a rock, piling large stones around it to secure it, and then flung the flag to the breeze.

I saw it was getting late and I made the best of my way back to the place where I had left my load. The descent was hard, as I have said, but the return was worse, and I was nearly exhausted before reaching the top. Selecting a good place near the "Cannon," I spent the next two hours in collecting wood, brush, and green spruce-trees; at the end of that time I had a very large pile under which I arranged the kindlings, and sat down to wait for the proper time to set the pile on fire. I determined to wait until nine o'clock, because many of the guests would then be in the piazza of the hotel, and also because the stages usually arrived about that time. It now occurred to me that I had not taken time to consider the enterprise carefully, in all its bearings, before starting.

There was no moon; I had omitted to bring a lantern, and I might find it difficult to get back, if I was obliged to stay out all night. To miss the path would be dangerous in the extreme, and to keep it in the darkness would be difficult. I might meet with the same mishap as that which happened in the year 1859 to Charles Barrett, a wealthy deaf-mute of Boston, now dead. He was one of a party of deaf-mutes who had been attending a Convention in Vermont, and were now visiting the Profile House. Most of them had made the ascent of Mount Lafayette, and they were seated around the fire after supper, enjoying themselves, when one of them suddenly asked what became of Mr. Barrett, who had not accompanied them up the Mountain. None of them had seen him since their return. Investigation proved that he was not about the hotel, but one of the servants remembered having seen him going up the path leading to the top of Cannon Mountain, and that he was alone. This caused instant alarm, and men were dispatched up the Mountain, with lanterns, to hunt for him. As the search progressed, his hat, cravat, coat, etc., were found in various places. He was finally found far out of the regular path, wandering aimlessly and distractedly about, and most completely lost. Before him, and directly in his way, was a steep precipice, and in all probability a few minutes' delay would have proved fatal. When he found that he was saved, his strength, which was nearly exhausted, gave way entirely, and he became unconscious. It was necessary to carry him most of the way back to the hotel, where a liberal use of restorative soon put him all right.

Having thought it all over, I concluded to carry out my original plan, and proceeded to eat my luncheon as a beginning. The wind in this elevated spot blew quite hard, and I felt chilly as my clothing was damp with perspiration. Finding a cleft in a rock which would protect me from the wind, I crept into it and remained two hours; the large bag in which I had brought the shavings served me as a shawl, and I was quite comfortable in body, although still somewhat uneasy in mind about getting down.

All was utter silence around me; the rapidly-increasing darkness, and the distance back, were not pleasant subjects for thought.

I was indeed, for the time, "monarch of all I surveyed"; but if my realm was limited by my vision, it was small indeed, and my crown by no means sat lightly on my brow. My watch finally told me, by the aid of a match, that it was nine o'clock, and I fired the pile; the wind fanned the flame to a huge blaze thirty feet or more in height, which illuminated the scene for miles around, and was quickly seen from the hotel. They told me afterwards that a cry of "fire" was raised, and every one of the three hundred and fifty persons then at the hotel was outside in a very few minutes, and enjoyed the scene very much. In about half an hour the fire died away; as soon as my eyes, which had been blinded by the blaze, became accustomed to the darkness, I set out to return; I could barely see to keep the path, and stumbled and fell quite often.

After a long and tedious journey, I arrived at the Profile House with no other damage than a bruised knee. The next morning inquiry was made about the fire, and a desire was expressed to see the person who made it; I was sent for and presented to the company, who, on being acquainted with the facts, made up a handsome contribution for me. The contribution was very welcome, I am free to say; but I do not think that I would do the same job over again for the same amount. A man will sometimes do a thing for his own gratification which he cannot afterward be hired to do at any price.

Going down to the lake, I was surprised to find that the pole was not on the Head, but some distance from it, among a group of rocks called "Adam's Apple." Not content to leave the job half done, I jumped into a boat, rowed across the lake, and struck off and up through the pathless woods to the pole, which I planted in another place. The Head was a very difficult and dangerous place to move or stand on. Returning to the lake, I found that the pole was in the right place.

In a few days, work was discontinued on the hotel, as the proprietors were obliged to give all their time to the rapidly-increasing number of guests, and I was dismissed, with orders to return after the travelling season was over. And so ended my first summer at the Mountains.

Second Summer

In General

THE TRAVELLING season at the Mountains begins about the last of June, or by the middle of July, and ends in September, or early in October. While at home, during the summer or fall, waiting the close of the travelling season, that I might return to the Mountains and watch the approach of winter, I laid my plans, and provided things which experience and observation had taught me were necessary in mountain wanderings: strong clothing, not easily torn by bushes and briars, through which I might have to force my way; a knapsack, drinking-flask, hand-axe, etc. I rejected the idea of a gun, as being both inconvenient and unnecessary. An axe, I thought, would serve all ordinary purposes of offence and defence, and in case of the appearance of a bear or other large animal, I could run away. My grandfather—a deaf-mute—used only to carry a hay-fork when he went after his cows, at a time when wild beasts were plenty; and he said he found it a very efficient weapon.

Orders at last came for me to return and resume work at the Profile House, and I accordingly departed for the Mountains, where, on my arrival, I received a hearty welcome.

The first thing I did after arriving there, was to hurry down to the spot from which the "Profile" can best be seen, and take a good look at my old friend, whose towering form loomed up in the gathering darkness like some grim sentinel standing guard over the forest. Having paid my respects to him, I returned, to the hotel, of which I will give a brief description.

It has four hundred windows, and can accommodate several hundred guests. It is built in the form of a cross, and stands on a level plain, a few acres in extent, surrounded on all sides by lofty mountains. Its front faces the Franconia Notch, through which the waters of the Echo and Profile Lakes flow into the Pemigewasset River, and thence into Lake Winnipisoegee. It is one of the most convenient, commodious, and best-managed hotels in the Mountains; it is within easy distance of some of the most interesting of the natural curiosities: Eagle Cliff, Echo and Profile Lakes, the Cascade and Falls, the "Old Man," the Basin, Pool, and Flume, Walker's Falls, and other minor objects. With its telegraph and stage offices, its hosts of servants and hundreds of guests, it is a town in itself. Immense quantities of provisions are consumed, and teams are constantly bringing the necessaries and luxuries of life over the Mountains from Littleton, eleven miles off. The establishment is supplied with pure mountain spring water, than which the world knows no better article. The stables are extensive, as the travel demands it, and I have often counted three hundred and fifty horses stabled at once.

Echo Lake

About three-fourths of a mile from the Profile House, nestling among the hills, and surrounded by a dense growth of trees, lies Echo Lake, a beautiful sheet of water, from which can be seen Eagle Cliff, Cannon Mountain, and Bald Mountain. It is remarkable for its echoes; the blowing of a tin horn, or shouting with the voice, will awake the "babbling gossips of the air," who will return the sounds with wonderful distinctness; the report of a swivel or gun fired in a certain direction, will reverberate like peals of thunder among the Mountains. All this I know only from hearsay, and walking the echoes is one of the few occasions on which I keenly feel my loss of hearing. The best time to visit the lake is near sunset—the magical beauty of the scene can then be best understood; and, if a man be in a meditative mood, there is no better place to "look through nature up to nature's God."

Take a boat and row to the middle of the lake, which is about one mile long and three-quarters of a mile wide, and of great depth and clearness, and, by looking down into the water, you can readily imagine yourself floating in mid-air.

I have twice stolen out at midnight, and paddled around the lake by moonlight. On one occasion, the report having spread that a bear and a deer had been seen at the farther end of the lake, my curiosity induced me to take a boat and go down to the place by moonlight, to see if anything was to be seen. Arriving there, I stepped on shore, advanced a few steps, and peered into the bushes. I could see nothing; and the perfect stillness around me, together with the strange hour, gave me a sudden panic, and I dashed into the boat and swept homeward with all possible speed.

The lake is a very popular resort, and parties often carry musical instruments out in the boats, the playing of which has a very fine effect. It is one of those places of which the more you see the more you wish to see.

Eagle Cliff

On the left of the Profile House is Eagle Cliff, a huge columnar crag, which towers far into the air, and seems almost to overhang the hotel, although it is in reality quite a distance off. Its top is a huge mass of jagged rocks, which leans over so much that it seems ready to fall from its place. The cliff derives its name from the fact that, high up on its face, and plainly visible from the hotel, there is a black-looking hole, where, for many years, a pair of eagles built their nest. Some mischievous persons went up one summer, with fire-arms, and frightened them away, much to the grief and indignation of the visitors, to whom the noble birds had afforded much gratification.

I have several times seen eagles sailing about the spot, and occasionally diving into the woods and then soaring away. I could not, from the distance, ascertain whether they obtained any prey, but was much interested in their movements, and wished for a nearer view. One day I was watching an eagle who had been hovering about the spot for some days, when I determined to get nearer, if possible. I plunged into the woods, and made my way as directly as I could towards the cliff. Reaching its foot, I commenced climbing up, taking care to keep out of sight of the eagle, who was now directly above me, sailing in a circle. I reached the foot of the crag, a distance of about three-quarters of a mile, after much exertion, and halted to rest. Through the branches above me I saw that the eagle had gone up higher, and I was afraid I had frightened him away. Wishing to get a better position, I crept cautiously on my hands and knees, and had nearly arrived at the place I wished, when I saw a plump rabbit sitting near its burrow. I sat down and watched it. In a few minutes I saw a dark object drop rapidly from the sky; the rabbit disappeared in its burrow; and the baffled eagle, for it was he, paused a moment, as if considering the situation, and then spreading his broad wings, he soared aloft again. He was only a short distance from me, and I had a splendid view of him. He was a noble specimen of the king of birds, with broad wings, heavy beak, and powerful claws. A momentary wish for a gun crossed my mind, but the next minute I was ashamed of myself, for it seemed almost a crime to shoot such a bird.

In about five minutes the rabbit appeared again, and almost at the same instant the eagle swept down, with a speed which set the bushes and leaves in motion like a breeze; and, grasping the unlucky rabbit in its claws, sailed gracefully away over the forest, and disappeared behind the cliff.

Before leaving the spot I took a survey of the rocks at the foot of the crag, and in one place I noticed a huge slab of rock standing on its edge, with a very slight hold on the face of the cliff. It had been loosened by frost, or other causes, and was evidently ready to slip or slide down the mountain by a very slight force. It would, I think, cover a quarter of an acre, and certainly weighed many tons.

The next spring, before the snow had quite disappeared, I was one day going to dinner with the rest of the workmen, when I suddenly felt a heavy jarring of the earth beneath my feet. At the same instant the man behind me gave me a heavy blow on the back, and when I turned sharply around, pointed to Eagle Cliff. I looked, and saw that the great slab before mentioned had got loose, and gone crashing and tearing to the foot of the Mountain. Deaf though I was, I was sensible of a terrible crash and an indescribable roaring. An immense column of smoke rose slowly up, and gradually disappeared.

The next morning I was one of a party who ascended to the spot where the slab had been. The immense mass of rock had cleared a path for itself for many rods below, sweeping the trees before it like chaff, and grinding some of them to powder. Rocks, large and small, were scattered far and wide, as they had been hurled from the path of the slab in its passage downward. I have seen snow-avalanches sweep down a mountain-side, and carry much before them, but this, being a solid mass of rock, far exceeded them in destructive force. I am inclined to think a number of such slides, at different periods, are what caused the outline of a human face known as "The Old Man," and I also think that, in time, other slides will occur which will entirely obliterate it. In my explorations over and upon the rocks which constitute the "Profile," I have noticed crevices and cracks in abundance, on which the action of frost and ice must eventually have a ruinous result. Of this I shall speak more fully hereafter, and shall also have more to say of Eagle Cliff, with which I afterwards became intimately acquainted.

Building a Boat-House

A boat-house being required at the Profile Lake, I was selected to build it. It was by no means a pleasant job, not on account of the work—that was easy enough—but by reason of the spot being just within the woods, which close down on the lake and swarm with midgets. These pests of the mountains often shorten the visits of tourists; they especially interfere with the labors of the artists, the enjoyment of the ramblers, and peace of everybody, everywhere, except in the hotels, their immediate vicinity, and some few other favored spots. I commenced operations, keeping up a fire to windward, and working in the smoke as best I might. From the spot where I worked I had a full view of the "Old Man," and, during the month that I was stationed there, I saw him in all the various aspects which the changes in the weather give him. My attention was divided between my work and the "Old Man" a good part of the time, and I often hit my fingers in the attempt to drive a nail and look the other way at once. Somehow, I could not help looking; the stern old face had a sort of fascination for me, and I almost worshipped it sometimes. Working at the lake, I had charge of the boats used by the guests of the hotel. One day I saw a stout old gentleman and three ladies coming towards the boats.

They stopped to enjoy the scenery for some time, and then the old gentleman called for me. I had my eyes on him, expecting to be spoken to, and I pointed to my ears and shook my head. He pointed to the boat, with a smile, and then to himself and party, signifying that he wanted one. I came down and cast one off for him; he stepped into it, stood erect, while the ladies took seats, and then throwing off his coat and gloves, he sat down, put out the oars, and sent the boat over the surface of the lake with a long, regular stroke, which showed him to be a sailor, and a man-of-war. In the course of an hour he returned, paid the customary fee, and went away. His bearing convinced me that he was no ordinary man. There were no signs of rank about him, only an indefinable something which created that impression. In the evening there was a ball, and I saw the old gentleman walking about with quite a crowd following, and learned that he was Admiral Farragut. I mentally did homage to the naval hero, and studied him with interest, during his stay in the grand parlor where the ball took place. The next day, while I was at work as usual, the Admiral came along, asked for slate and pencil, and engaged me in conversation in regard to the circumstances attending my visit to the "Old Man," while I was constructing my "model"; a copy of which, hanging in the hotel, had attracted his attention on the previous evening. In regard to my exploration on the dizzy heights of the "Profile," the Admiral asked me if I was not afraid at the time; to which, Yankee-like, I replied by asking him if he was not afraid when he stood in the shrouds of his vessel at the capture of New Orleans? He incidentally remarked that he was acquainted with the veteran Laurent Clerc, who came from France, the first instructor of deaf-mutes in America, and others of our notable men.

At the close of the interview I felt much elated by having had a personal conversation, all to myself, with the hero of New Orleans. There was nothing remarkable, to be sure, in his talking with me as he did; but in my regard to the fact as one of the events of my life, I am no more absurd, to say the least, than are the multitudes who throng wherever our great statesmen and generals happen to sojourn, and crowd and elbow each other in desperate eagerness to get a sight of the man or a shake of his hand. The Admiral impressed me as a dignified, but genial old man, with nothing of the aristocrat about him—a genuine son of the sea—fond of society, and carrying with him a certain air, which, while conducive to social intercourse, repelled any approach to familiarity. I hoped to see him again, but when I returned from my work at night, I learned that he was gone. I saw him, some time afterward, in the Railroad Station, at Hartford, Conn., and had the pleasure of being recognized, and getting a shake of his hand, just as he stepped on board of a train. He stands high in my estimation of men, and, hero-worship or not, I say: Long live Admiral Farragut.

A Week with a Photographer

There came to the Profile House a seedy-looking man, whose baggage was two heavy chests, and who, as we soon discovered, was a photographer, sent by a firm in New York to take views of the places of interest in the Mountains. He was not a very prepossessing individual; wore an army uniform, and had only one eye, black and piercing, but we were soon interested in him. We learned that he went out with Dr. Kane's expedition in search of Sir John Franklin, as a photographer, but the intense cold prevented him from taking views, and he was otherwise employed. He had been in the army during our civil war, and a splinter destroyed one of his eyes at the battle of Malvern Hill.

He had come to the Mountains at the wrong time, July and August being the best months for photographing. He remained over a week without seeing a single fair day, and was almost in despair. He wished to engage me to guide and assist him in taking views, at the first opportunity, and I obtained permission to help him for a week. He wished to go to some parts of the Mountains which had never been visited by photographers.

We loaded ourselves with his apparatus and other necessary articles, and went here and there for some time with varied success. He at last decided to ascend Eagle Cliff, and try to get views of the Profile House and the surrounding scenery.

Our loads weighed over a hundred pounds each, and the ascent was hard indeed, but we finally reached the spot where I had watched the eagle, as related before. We cut down several trees, made a clearing, and built a staging about six feet high, from which a wide view could be had. He succeeded, in taking several good pictures.

The next day we talked it over, and determined to camp out two days. Taking our loads, as before, with provisions enough to last until our return, we proceeded to the "Basin," taking views on the way.

The "Basin" is a deep hollow worn in the solid granite by the long-continued action of the water, which falls into it over a ledge a few feet in height, and escapes through a small, opening at the opposite side. Its shortest width is twenty feet, and its depth fifteen feet. It forms a mammoth bowl, which is always filled with very cold and pure water. The water is very clear, and the bottom can be distinctly seen. Viewed from a certain spot on one side, the other side assumes the form of a gigantic foot, with the sole outward, and fully exposed to the action of the water. It is a beautiful place, close to the road, and it is pleasant to linger there and watch the eddying whirl of waters.

At the Basin we determined to remain all day and night. After taking a few views in different positions, in each of which I figured, the photographer removed his apparatus to the other side, and had got it adjusted, when he hit one leg of the stand with his foot and sent the whole into the Basin. In trying to save it, he slipped, and fell in himself. I was standing near him, and, knowing that he could not swim, I made such haste to catch him that I, too, went headlong into the water. The water was icy cold, it being near November. Being a good swimmer, I soon placed my companion where he could hold on for a few minutes, and having got out myself, I helped him to do the same. We were in a bad way, certainly; both of us wet to the skin, and the apparatus fifteen feet under water. The poor fellow actually wept, believing he had lost it forever; but I told him I would get it again, even if I had to dive for it. Procuring a long pole, we made a very good grappling with some nails we had with us, and let it down, but found it too short. Splicing it with cords, we again let it down, and, as I was feeling about for the object of our search, I lost my balance and fell into the Basin a second time. I had, at previous times, like many others, stood on the brink of the Basin, and longed for a plunge in the "delicious-looking bath"; but I changed my mind entirely after this second experience, and at all subsequent visits to the spot, I "looked but longed no more." Undaunted, I climbed out, and we renewed our attempts to recover the apparatus, which we finally succeeded in doing.

Oh! How we capered and laughed, forgetting that we were thoroughly wet, two miles from any house, and without the means to make a fire. By the time that we began to realize our situation, and consider what we should do, a team happened along and we procured some matches of the driver, and determined to stay all night, as we had at first intended. We built a large fire, and so far dried our clothes that we felt comfortable, and then worked on till near sundown, when we looked about for a place to spend the night. I remembered having seen a small shanty, somewhere in the vicinity, a year before, and went to look for it. After a diligent search, I found it about half a mile away, and returned to guide my comrade to it, marking the trees as I went, to insure a speedy return. It was the best place we could find; and we proceeded to make ourselves comfortable, although the fact that there was an old bear-trap near by, brought up rather unpleasant associations; the idea of one of those animals coming along, not being agreeable.

We ate our supper cold, and made our bed with moss and blankets. We were afraid to build a fire in that place, for fear of a conflagration in the woods, a thing which had happened before from the same cause. The gloom of the forest, and the rapidly-increasing darkness, were indeed thrilling. The darkness put it out of our power to converse, which was rather uncomfortable. All was utter silence to me; my companion doing the hearing for both of us, while, I suppose, I did my share of the thinking. Neither of us slept much that night, the strangeness of my position and my own thoughts keeping me awake; while the rustling of swaying branches, the voice of falling waters, and the hooting of owls, made it impossible for him to sleep. He told me afterward, that the owls scared him badly; and I confessed that my imagination conjured up so many bears, snakes, and other denizens of the forest, that I was heartily glad when morning came. At day-break my companion fell asleep, and remained so, until a large owl, of which I had a good view, awakened him by its hooting, when I told him to keep watch, and was soon asleep, careless whether he obeyed orders or not.

Refreshed by our naps, we ate our breakfasts and returned to the Basin, from which we went to the Pool, but were unable to take any views, on account of cloudy weather. We took lodgings at the Flume House, and the next day, after obtaining views of the Flume, we commenced our return.

Arriving at the foot of Mount Lafayette, we halted, and held a consultation as to the possible advantage of ascending it, and the probability of being able to obtain views from its summit. It was late in the season, and the ascent was dangerous, on account of the frost-clouds, to be caught in one of which is almost certain death.

I had ventured up, a few days before, at a time when there was a dense frost-cloud, and all the trees above were covered with a white and glistening coat of frost. I wanted to *feel* how cold it was, and to ascertain how far I could endure it. (The reader will observe, that to go up when a frost-cloud is abroad, and approach it from below, is a very different thing from having one sweep down upon, and envelope, the unfortunate person who happens to be in the way. In the former case, one can retreat at pleasure; in the latter, one seldom escapes with life.) I carried with me overcoat and mittens, which I did not need to put on for some time, it being a warm day. As I approached the border of the frost-cloud, I put them on, and ventured some distance up. I *felt* it, sure enough. It was a stinging, suffocating cold; the air was filled with minute particles of frozen mist, and my hair and beard were quickly white; while my clothes, before I left, were frozen stiff. When I could bear the cold no longer, I beat a retreat.

I noticed a very singular thing during my stay: The wind was blowing quite hard, and the particles of mist or frost, clinging to the trees and to each other, made icicles, which did not hang down as we generally see them, but stood out horizontally from trees, rocks, stumps, etc., giving the whole a very striking appearance.

As I descended to warmer regions, the heat gradually thawed out my frozen clothes; and when I arrived at the foot of the mountain, I was as wet as if I had been plunged under water. It will now be seen how dangerous it was for us to venture up. If we reached the top, and a frost-cloud should be seen coming, we could not possibly reach a place of safety with our loads. We finally decided to make the attempt.

The photographer and myself slowly ascended with our heavy loads, keeping a sharp look-out, after leaving the line of the forest, for any appearance of danger. As we neared the top of the Mountain we saw a spot of cloud afar off, which I knew was a sign of the approach of the frost-demon, and we turned and rapidly made our way back, narrowly escaping the deadly embraces of the cloud, so speedily did it sweep after us. Of course, all our labor was lost; taking views was impossible. We gave up the attempt, and returned to the Profile House. The next day we made an equally fruitless ascent of Cannon Mountain; after which, the prospect was so bad that my photographing friend gave up the job, packed his things, bade farewell to the Mountains, and returned to New York.

A Deaf and Dumb Guide Better Than None

Soon after the departure of my friend the one-eyed photograph man, a gentleman made his appearance at the Profile House, who hailed from New Jersey. He came very late, as the season had closed to all intents and purposes, and only a few stragglers remained of the swarm of visitors. He inquired for a Guide, and was told that the regular Guides had all gone home, but that I would make a good one, as I was well acquainted with the Mountains, and had served in that capacity before. On learning that I was deaf and dumb; he flatly refused to take me, adding some very uncomplimentary remarks, which were reported to me, of which I took no apparent notice, although I made a memorandum of them in my mind. One day he ventured out alone in search of Walker's Falls, of which I shall have more to say hereafter. It was in the afternoon, and the hill-tops were enveloped in clouds. The distance to the Falls, from the road leading to the Flume House, is one mile and a-half. Neglect and mountain storms had nearly obliterated that half of the path nearest the Falls, making it easy to lose one's way. At sundown, the gentleman had not returned, and an alarm was raised. I was requested to go in search of him, and at once consented, glad of the chance to show him that his estimation of a Deaf and Dumb was wrong; and I started off alone. After leaving the road, I soon found his trail in the soft moss, it retaining the impression of a person's foot for a long time; and pursued it with all possible haste, as the dusk was coming on and time was precious.

It was necessary for me to keep directly on the trail, and I, being deaf, might pass quite near him without seeing him, and he might not see or hear me. I found, by the direction of his trail, that he had gone wrong, and could not possibly have reached the Falls. I found him perched on a rock, wiping his brow vigorously. He had given himself up for lost, and his conduct, when he saw me, somewhat belied his previously-expressed opinion of a deaf-mute guide. He caught my hand and shook it warmly. We had no time to waste in words, and if we had, it was too dark to write, by which method only could we communicate.

Beckoning him to follow, I took the back track, and went forward at a rapid rate, up hill and down, over rocks and stumps, through bushes and briars, intent on gaining the main road before utter darkness came on. He came after me, panting and perspiring, frequently stumbling over some obstacles, and falling headlong; and, plainly objecting to such rapid locomotion, I confess to having experienced a sort of malicious pleasure in leading him such a race, in consideration of his remarks on me the other day. After a while I became slightly anxious, as the darkness increased, lest we should miss the way; but while turning it over in my mind, we burst through a clump of bushes, directly into the road, and I shortly had the pleasure of seeing him safe in the arms of his anxious wife.

For the rest of his stay, he employed me as his guide, paying me liberally; besides stating, at the close of my engagement, that, although he had travelled much, both in the old world and the new, he had never had a better guide.

My Ascent of Mount Lafayette

The most remarkable sight I had ever witnessed, occurred one afternoon this season. The clouds were gathering, and slowly descending, and there was every appearance of a rain-storm, when I determined to venture up the Mountain, to see whether it was clear at the top. I hurried up as fast as I could, and having made the ascent, passing through a dense cloud on my way, I was rewarded by a singular sight. Below me, and shutting off all other view, was, apparently, a thick field of cotton, almost tempting me to jump into its soft folds. I learned, afterward, that soon after my departure from the hotel it commenced raining heavily, and the people there thought I was in a bad plight for venturing on the Mountain at such an improper time. They did not appreciate my love of adventure, and my desire to experience the sensation of being above a storm-cloud. I had often read of persons standing on the top of a mountain while there was a storm raging below them, and I now felt quite elated at my good fortune in witnessing a similar scene.

Very soon the cotton-cloud changed to a bright red color, as if on fire, caught from the sun, which was shining brightly above. The scene now became sublime, beyond my ability to describe. I was reminded of the Israelites fleeing from Egypt, guided by a pillar of fire by night. For many miles around, this magnificent sight met my eye. Soon, however, I noticed that the cloud was rising, which made me feel quite uneasy, for fear that I should get a thorough soaking, which would render me quite uncomfortable, and perhaps place me in a dangerous plight from the cold and wet, and there was no chance for escape; so I had to content myself by waiting its approach. I saw no lightning, nor did I feel any jar from the thunder, in which I was somewhat disappointed. As the cloud arose, I was agreeably surprised to find that it did not rain at all, but there was a thick mist or cloud rising fast, and in a few minutes it had passed above my head, slowly uniting, until it appeared like a great white cloth or sheet spread over many miles around. The whole Mountain range came into full view, in all its grandeur and majesty.

I was riveted to the spot in amazement at this unexpected scene, and I can hardly find words to portray the beautiful spectacle. The rising of a mammoth curtain in a mammoth theatre, might give some idea of what I beheld coming into view: a grand panorama of splendid and varied landscape. Mount

Washington, thirty miles away, revealed itself in mighty grandeur, with all its surroundings of minor hills. But the descending sun warned me not to tarry, but to hasten down while yet there was daylight enough to guide my steps. I found most of the path very wet and muddy, but reached the hotel without harm.

A Party Overwhelmed by a Severe Rain-Storm

To show the danger there is in incautiously attempting an ascent of the Mountains, I will narrate an incident that occurred in the early part of this season.

A party of five gentlemen and five ladies determined to risk the ascent of Mount Lafayette quite early, being, I think, the first party of the season, notwithstanding the remonstrances of the hotel-keeper. The weather appeared quite unpromising, but, having a guide, they ventured off, and reached the top of the Mountain without particular adventure. They had hardly dismounted, and taken a view of the scene before them, when they were surrounded by a dense cloud, which totally obscured their vision. Quickly mounting their horses, they had gone but a few rods when a heavy rain-storm burst upon them, forming a torrent, which filled the path so that they could not find their way.

The horses refused to move, being frightened and bewildered, and even a hard beating had no effect upon them. The whole party was in a very dangerous plight, for they were pitiable-looking objects, completely drenched; and the ladies looked most miserable, helpless, and trembling with fear and the cold. They were held on to the horses by the gentlemen accompanying them, or they would have fallen exhausted to the ground. The rain poured in ceaseless torrents, as if from sheer malice, to punish the imprudent adventurers.

There was great consternation at the hotel when the storm came on, as it seemed unlikely that any of the party could survive its chilling effects. A quick consultation was had, and volunteers called for to go to the rescue. I quickly offered my services; and six others following my example, we hastily procured a two-horse carriage, and drove with great speed the three miles to the foot of the Mountain. Here we unharnessed the horses from the carriage, tying them, so they should not stray, and proceeded on foot up the Mountain, which we did with great difficulty, discomfort, and danger, the path being filled with water, and the pelting rain nearly blinding us. Finally, we reached the spot where the party stood, more dead than alive, and truly pitiable objects to behold. We did not stop to ask any questions, but quickly got the ladies off the horses, gave them a drink of something which the strictest teetotaller would probably not have denied them under the circumstances, and then each took one of the ladies and started down the Mountain again, the gentlemen gladly following with all possible speed. The horses were also induced to move, and when we got half way down, and had partially revived the almost perishing party, we again mounted them on their horses, putting a man on each side to hold them in place. By dint of great caution, we finally reached the carriage, into which we placed the ladies, letting their horses gallop off towards home. Again harnessing our horses to the carriage, we started off with all speed to the hotel, where we arrived without further mishap. The travelling party received prompt aid and by careful nursing, and the use of proper stimulants, they were fortunately able to be about the next morning, apparently none the worse for their dangerous predicament.

The Adventurous Little Girl

One Sunday afternoon, a little waiter-girl, not more than eleven years old, banteringly said that she would ascend Mount Lafayette alone, if no one would accompany her. Some of the older boys, who were fond of mischief, wishing to see some fun, and to test her strength, offered to go with her, promising help, if necessary, in the ascent and descent.

So off they started to the foot of the Mountain, without the knowledge of any older persons. The ascent was very difficult for one so young; she started up very courageously, but her strength not being equal to the task, she soon faltered; but the boys cruelly drove her up, by threats. She often wavered, but finally was enabled to nearly reach the top, a distance of about three miles from the foot of the Mountain. Here her tired limbs refused any longer to sustain her, and she fell, exhausted, to the ground.

The boys became quite alarmed at this result of their persuasion and threats, and, finding that the sun was getting well down, they became frightened, for fear that they should all perish with the cold at night.

One of the oldest, more courageous than the rest, offered to stay with the little girl while the rest should hasten back for help. Arriving at the hotel, they quickly gave the alarm, and men were dispatched for the little adventurer. She was brought down the Mountain more dead than alive, having fearful spasms, and reached the hotel utterly exhausted. A messenger was sent five miles for a doctor, by whose care she was revived, but without any particular desire to try such a jaunt again. It is, perhaps, needless to say, that the boys were more careful afterward, heartily thankful that no ill effects followed their fool-hardiness.

Taking the Measure of the Old Man of the Mountain

One day, while looking at the stucco-workers at the hotel, the idea struck me that a *fac-simile* of the "Old Man of the Mountain" might be made of Calcined Plaster. This *was* an idea which promised large rewards if it could be accomplished. But how to get an exact counterfeit presentment of His High Mightiness, *that* was the question. Cheered with the hope of success, I soon had my wits at work determining how to get at the measurements of the various rocks which combine to make up this wonderful profile. I was satisfied that it would take many weary hours of toil and danger to accomplish the task I had laid out for myself, but I was determined to succeed, and *I did*.

Preparing a clothes-line forty feet long, and a piece of white cotton cloth about four feet square, to the top and bottom of which I fastened heavy pieces of wood, so that their weight should keep the cloth smooth when spread out and suspended. One morning, without informing any one of my intention, I started quite early, taking along the line and cloth, not forgetting a lunch, and my little hatchet, and made the ascent directly from the Bowling Alley, straight to the Face, instead of by the ordinary path. The ascent was very difficult and dangerous, and I was very much fatigued, but finally succeeded in gaining the top.

After careful examination below, I reached the top of the head, and having attached my cloth to the line, I lowered it over the face, and fastened it in a crack in the rock. I could not see where it landed; so, after partaking of my lunch, I started back down the Mountain, being obliged to go to a point eighty rods beyond the hotel, in order to see where the cloth had rested. I found that it had landed on the nose, and, as that was one-half the height of the whole profile, I knew that the entire height must be *eighty feet*, or twice the length of my forty-foot line.

While I was still looking up at the face, some one gave the alarm at the hotel, that some vandal had painted a white spot on the Old Man's nose, and quite spoiled his beauty. The hotel-keeper sent his clerk to ascertain what had been done, and to stop further depredations. Finding me intently watching the head, he presumed at once that I was the mischief-maker; he shook his fist at me, and then asked me, in writing, why I painted that spot on the nose? I laughed outright; and soon mollified him by telling him that it was impossible for any live man to get upon the nose. I then explained my object, and the means of obtaining the correct distances for the proposed *fac-simile*. He then returned to the hotel, and reported to the proprietor, who afterward desired me to be quick, and remove the unsightly spot.

So, early the next morning, I again ascended the Mountain, this time in a dense cloud; and having removed the cloth, returned to the hotel in season for breakfast.

The visit to the head was repeated in a few days, and I then even ventured, more than once, *under the chin*, which proved extremely hazardous; and, but for my determination to get an accurate measurement, would have been quickly abandoned, as too risky for mortal man to undertake. I was told that no man had ever been known to go there before; but, whether true or not, I do not intend ever to risk my wife's husband's neck on any such desperate errand again; all the money in Wall Street would now be no allurement. I accomplished my task, and succeeded in getting, by various methods, the exact size and form of the various features which combine to form this most wonderful profile.

When I reported this last part of the adventure, no one was willing to believe that I had really been under the chin. Finding them so faithless, I offered to go once more, and prove my presence by building a fire under the chin, the smoke of which would be visible from the road. This I did; and then returning, without serious suffering, I was welcomed with amazement.

The spot I reached was directly under the chin, about twenty feet below it. If it had been possible to take along a short ladder, I could have gained foothold on a small projection, and touched the chin, which was about fifteen feet from the top to the neck, but it would have been extremely hazardous; for, if I had tripped ever so little, and lost my balance, I should have gone down the cliff some two thousand feet, and been dashed to pieces on the ragged rocks below. In case of such a termination, it is not likely that these sketches would ever have seen the light; and, after considering the matter of late, I am rather glad that I was preserved from falling.

I was very successful in making the desired model, and produced a truthful representation of the "Great Stone Face" for which I received the highest praise, and of which I made and sold a large number of copies.

The successful accomplishment of this undertaking rendered me quite famous in the Mountain region and there are many who visited the Mountains that year, who greatly assisted me in disposing of copies of the model. Among these was one of the editors of the New York *Journal of Commerce*, who gave me a "first-rate notice" in his gigantic newspaper, from which I extract the following:

"Mr. Wm. B. Swett, an ingenious deaf-mute, who has been employed for several summers at the Profile House, in the Franconia Mountains, and who is noted for his many adventures among them, produced, during the summer of 1866, a remarkable work—a *fac-simile* of the Great Stone Face.

"It was made from actual measurement; taken at great risk of life and limb, he having been on the brow five times, and is said to be the first, and perhaps the only man, who ever ventured under the Chin, to get a correct view of the rocks which constitute the face.

"The fact is not generally known, that the 'Profile' is produced, not by the edge of one rock, but by the accidental grouping of a number of rocks, at various distances from each other.

"The front of the top of the precipice, which is about sixteen hundred feet high, is a group of rocks one hundred feet in breadth, and eighty feet high. The Nose is forty feet from the Forehead. The Mouth, which seems an opening of two thin lips, is a side-long chasm, or break, of fifty feet in extent.

"Viewed from the front, the Profile disappears, and can, indeed, only be seen from one point."

The Panther and Indian on Eagle Cliff

Always on the look-out for opportunities to make a sensation, and add to the attraction of the localities, both for my own profit and that of the proprietors, I conceived the idea of placing a wooden panther high up on Eagle Cliff, facing the hotel.

After frequent visits to the Cliff, for the purpose of selecting a good place, and of calculating the distance, I went to work on my model.

Aware that "distance lends enchantment to views," I drew the outlines roughly, and made it eighteen feet long, and large in proportion. It represented the animal in a crouching attitude, ready for a spring. I made it in nine pieces, using pine plank, one inch thick, for the purpose. Having matched and painted, or daubed these pieces to my satisfaction, I made nine secret visits to the selected spot, to which I had previously "blazed" a path, carrying one piece each time; I secreted the pieces in the bushes, and waited for the proper time. When the hotel was well filled with guests, myself and a boy went up one morning at three o'clock, and put the model together, nailing it firmly to trees, and bracing it well. The location was the brink of a precipice; and, during erection, I had to crawl around on its very edge, where there was so little foot-hold that I had a rope around my waist, the other end of which was lashed to a tree. After the model was up, it looked so rough and uncouth that I began to have misgivings as to the effect from the hotel; and having given it a few more daubs of paint, I hurried back, anxious to get the first view of it from the place. It was not yet six o'clock, and no one had yet appeared. Having assured myself that the model was lightly placed, looked quite natural, and could not fail to be noticed, I retired, to watch the effect, feeling highly gratified with my success. Some early risers soon appeared on the piazza, stretching themselves, rubbing their eyes, and expanding their lungs with copious inhalations of the keen, pure, and bracing Mountain air. Having cleared the night-mists from eye and brain, they proceeded to enjoy the prospect. One of them, looking in the direction of the Cliff, suddenly started, rubbed his eyes, and looked again, to be sure he was not deceived, and called the attention of the next to the model. Instantly, all was excitement; the more casual spectators apparently taking it for a reality, and the cry of "a panther! a panther!!" which rang through the house, soon brought all who were about to the piazza and front yard; while those yet in their rooms threw up their windows, and looked eagerly forth; telescopes and opera-glasses were brought into requisition, and soon settled the nature of the object, after which, the guests began to speculate as to the author of this exploit. The editor of the New York *Journal of Commerce*, who had some previous knowledge of me, decided that it must be my doing. He hunted me up, and asked me about it. I told him the whole story; whereupon he took me with him, and introduced me to the crowd, who listened with interest to his repetition of my story, voted the deed a success, and made up a handsome purse, which was presented to me as a token of their appreciation.

The next spring I returned, and found the panther still in its place. A visit to the spot proved it to be uninjured by the storms of the past winter, and I determined to put up the figure of an Indian with a gun, in the act of shooting the panther. I made the figure and the gun out the same material I had used in constructing the panther—inch-pine lumber.

The Indian was twenty feet high, and his gun was sixteen feet long, the barrel being eight inches wide. When I got the thing ready, I was very weak, from the effects of a bad cold, and was unable to conduct my operations as secretly as before. I, however, communicated my project to as few persons as possible, and got a gang of ten men to carry the pieces and the necessary implements, while I went with them to guide them to the spot, and to superintend operations. The day was hot, and the ascent rough, so that I was soon exhausted and had to be helped on the way. Long before we arrived at our destination, I was almost dead for want of a drink of water. We had brought none with us, but discovered a place where water was oozing from the face of the rock. It did not come fast enough to give me a drink, and it was thinly spread over so much surface that I could only moisten my parched lip and tongue. Taking a bag, which I had with me, I half filled it, with the soft moss of the forest; and, by pressing the bag against the face of the rock, absorbed all the water that came. When the bag, by its increased weight, appeared to contain a sufficient quantity, I applied my mouth to a corner, compressed the bag with my hands, and obtained a copious and delicious draught. Having satisfied my thirst, I again applied the bag to the rock, filled it as full as possible, and resumed the ascent. The bag furnished several refreshing draughts of water before we reached the desired place. It was necessary to locate the Indian at a considerable distance from the panther, in order to secure the proper effect; and, as we could not see the latter, it required several trips to and fro, and some nice calculations; but we finally got it right, as observation from the hotel afterwards proved. Having nailed it to the trees, and braced it firmly, we returned to the Profile House, where the guests showed their appreciation of the enterprise by a second liberal collection. At latest accounts during the summer of 1869, the panther and Indian still remained.

A Perilous Adventure

One Saturday noon, after dinner, the other workmen and my-self were outside of the hotel, chatting and smoking, before re-suming work, when one of them asked me, in a bantering way, if I could ascend Eagle Cliff directly from the hotel, instead of taking the usual roundabout way. After some hesitation, I said I could do it, and would go if I could get permission to leave work, and that I would fling out a white flag at the top. All the lumber which we used had to be brought over the Mountains on teams, and it was slow and tedious work. This was before the idea occurred to the proprietors to build a steam saw-mill, which was afterwards done, and from which an ample supply was furnished. As we happened to be out of lumber at the time, I readily obtained leave of absence.

Procuring a table-cloth and some stout twine, and taking neither coat, axe, or lunch, as usual—so confident was I that I should need none of them—I plunged into the woods, about two o'clock, P.M., and commenced the ascent. The day was warm; the work uncomfortable; and the midgets, or wood-flies, more troublesome than ever. I had to keep my hands constantly in motion about my face to keep them off; their bite being always annoying, and often poisonous. The ascent became more and more difficult, and I made up my mind that it was a mad work to get to the top; but, to think of return-ing, was not pleasant, as the boys would laugh at me. I might take the usual way, and no one be the wiser; but that would be a cheat, and so I kept on. I had often to scramble up on my hands and knees, and to pull myself up by roots and bushes, and be very cautious about it, as they had no firm hold in the ground, and were easily pulled up. A bush suddenly gave way in one place, and, had not a large tree prevented it, I should have had a serious fall upon the jagged rocks twenty feet be-low. It was now impossible to descend, for I was on a ledge from which no downward path was visible. Working my way up, with immense labor, I at last discovered a huge crack or fissure, some thirty feet long, two feet wide, and ten feet high, with several trees growing in it, and I squeezed myself up and through it. At its end I was glad to see that I was near the top, which I quickly gained. While resting from the fatigue induced by my exertions, I was troubled with unpleasant doubts about a safe return; but I dismissed them for the present, and, climbing the tallest tree I could find, I obtained a truly sublime view. The tree waved gently to and fro in the wind with a soothing effect; Lafayette lifted itself far toward the sky, and far below me was the Profile House, looking no larger than a birdhouse, such as are often set up by boys. I longed to have some of my friends present to share my delight. I tied the table-cloth out on the branches, and immediately the guests and workmen began to congregate in front of the hotel, and to wave their handkerchiefs, to show that they saw that I had really reached the top, although they probably had not expected to see me make my appearance in the top of a tree. Descending from the tree, after an hour of true enjoyment, I was soon convinced that it was impossible to return by the way I had come, and that my only course was to make the best of my way to the columnar crag, and search for a path down its side. The distance was only half a mile, but the undergrowth was so thick, and fallen trees so numerous, that my progress was very slow. I now repented not having brought my hand-axe, with which to cut my way through. The pitiless midgets followed me in clouds; I never smoke, or I could easily have kept them off. I have tried mosquito-netting around my head and face, but found it to answer no good purpose, as, besides being easily torn, it interfered with the frequent necessity of wiping away the perspiration, and was otherwise uncomfortable.

From the blink of the crag, to which I finally attained, I had another glorious view of the hills; a small part of the chin of the

"Old Man" could be seen, but nothing of the nose, mouth, or forehead. I built a small fire in a hole in the rock, both to drive off the midgets and attract the attention of those below. The crowd soon saw the smoke, and the waving of handkerchiefs was repeated. I had stepped on a piece of rock to have a better view, and, as I turned to get down, I felt it move; with a sudden spring, I grasped a bush, and fell flat upon my breast, while the stone rolled over, and went thundering down the precipice. I wished to get down the cliff, it is true, but not in that hasty fashion, as I came near doing. Putting out the fire, a precaution the importance of which I would impress upon all who build fires in the woods, the neglect of it having caused many extensive conflagrations, I resumed my search for a way down. During this time, a pair of large owls flew up from the depths below, fluttered blindly about for a moment or two, and then dove down again. I am not superstitious, otherwise the appearance of these birds, considered of evil omen, at such a time and place, might have depressed my already heavy spirits. After a long search, I found I was in a tight place, and saw no other way out of it than to go down the opposite side of the cliff, and ascend Mount Lafayette.

Viewed from a distance, the deep, black ravine that scars the Mountain-side seemed easy of ascent; a complete deception, as will be seen. Once at the top of the ravine, I could easily gain the well-known bridle-path, and from that point the way was clear. I should also have another extensive view, and it was rare for one to get three different views, from points so far apart, on the same day. I was admonished to make haste, as the sun, considering the distance I had yet to go and the probable and possible difficulties of the way, was unpleasantly near setting.

I ran, jumped and slid as far as the bottom of the valley, where I stopped to quench my thirst in a clear, sparkling brook which ran there, built a fire to keep the midgets away, and sat down to rest a little, contemplating, meanwhile, the yawning blackness of the ravine, which was now directly in front of me, and looked gloomy enough, but its very gloom was sublime.

As soon as I got well rested, I commenced the ascent in earnest. I was frequently obliged to cross and re-cross the rushing brook; the sides were very steep, and trees and bushes were scattered here and there, but the ravine was mostly lined, as far as one could see, with large and small stones, from which the rains had washed away the earth, until many of them stood ready to roll down at a touch, or even at a heavy jar. The sun shone straight into the chasm, and the lofty sides kept the wind away; the heat was almost suffocating, and before long most of my clothing was saturated with perspiration. The ascent, comparatively easy at first, became more difficult every moment, and the heat more oppressive; to think of stopping was out of the question, as eight miles still lay between myself and the Profile House. Detention, by darkness, would very likely be death. I could not shorten the distance by climbing the side, for the underbrush was impenetrable without an axe. So I pushed along, painfully; I was much fatigued and excited; my feet were sore; the soles of my shoes, new the day before, being worn through. I began to fear I could not extricate myself from the ravine, and I prayed for deliverance as I had never prayed before; thoughts of my family, and of my past life, flashed through my mind.

It is remarkable how rapidly and clearly a man can think when in danger; in what a short space of time every act of his life, good or bad, passes in review before him. About this time, I stepped on a loose rock, which slid from under my feet, and rolled heavily downward, starting numerous other rocks in its course, and raising an immense cloud of dust. I soon discovered a new source of danger; the jar, and the reverberations of the rolling stones below me, had started those above, and they now rolled past in considerable numbers, some of them passing quite near me. The rock on which I now stood—to which I had sprung when the other gave way—was quite slippery, and I could not move out of the way should any of the stones come in my direction, lest I lose my footing and follow them to the bottom.

The ravine above and ahead of me was steep, and quite smooth. Looking up, to see how long the commotion was likely to last, I saw a huge rock far up the slope, coming directly down upon me at a fearful speed. I also noticed that a large rock cropped out ten or twelve feet above my head, and that the coming stone would hit it, and, in all probability, fetch both upon me, and hurl me to destruction. Mentally bidding farewell to the world, and commending my spirit to God, I kept my eyes fixed on the rock. It struck the projection—which proved to be a solid spur in the Mountain-side, and consequently did not move—bounded over my head, and went spinning to the bottom, where it flew into a thousand pieces.

A few more stones passed me, and then all became quiet again. I cannot describe my feelings at this deliverance; but I imagine I know how a man feels who has been reprieved at the foot of the gallows.

I now took courage, and resumed the ascent, picking my way up carefully. Farther on, I came to a broad, flat rock, steep, wet and slippery. Being unable to go around it on either side, I went down on hands and knees and crawled up its surface. Reaching what I thought a safe place, I attempted to stand upright. My feet slipped, and I fell on my face, bruising myself considerably. I slid on and down till my eye caught a little crack in the rock, into which I got the ends of my fingers, and thus stopped the descent, though it seemed only a postponement of the inevitable end; for of course I could not hold on forever. I could not move; the clouds of midgets which had followed me all along, now seemed to know that their opportunity had come, and settled in a mass on my neck, face and hands. The torment was terrible, but I was helpless.

Over the surface of the rock on which I was spread out, the water trickled from a spring above, and I was soon quite wet. If I was obliged to stay out all night, my only safety was in having a good fire. Since leaving the last place where I had made a fire, I had discovered that I laid my matches on the ground, while lighting it, and left them there; and that I had but one solitary match, which was in my vest pocket. My greatest fear now was, that this one match would get wet, and I be thus reduced to extremity.

Looking carefully around, I saw a crevice, not far from my feet, into which, if I could get my feet, I could resume my progress on hands and knees. The length of my legs, inconvenient at times, now did me good service, as they could just reach it. Cautiously letting go my hold with one hand, and finding it was safe, I indulged in a savage sweep at the midgets on my face, giving me a slight relief. A little exertion enabled me to get out of my dangerous situation, crawl away, continue my upward progress, and reach the strange-looking rock near the top of the Mountain, known as the "Altar," where I dropped on the moss, utterly exhausted, but very thankful that the worst was over.

A little dirty water helped to revive me. The sun was near setting—it had set long ago to those in the valleys below—and the air, clearer than at any of my previous visits, afforded me a most magnificent view, the beauty of which chained me to my seat, till the light began to fade away. My one match proved to have fortunately remained unwet, and the descent of the Mountain, by the bridle-path, now began.

The sharp stones hurt my feet, and my progress was not rapid; when the woods below the cone of the Mountain were reached, the darkness rendered further progress dangerous without a light; the idea of a night in the woods was rejected; a pile of white birch-bark was collected, and a torch made; the one match, upon the ignition of which so much depended, was drawn, with a prayer for success; the torch blazed forth, and by its light the foot of the Mountain was reached at last. Then followed a long rest on the grass at the side of the road, rendered doubly sweet by a knowledge that the danger was passed, and only two miles of smooth travel now intervened.

The hotel was finally reached, and it is doubted if a more famished tatterdemalion was ever seen within its walls than entered them about ten o'clock that night, and sank helplessly on a chair.

My entrance cut short the speculations, and allayed the anxieties, of all concerned. Every attention was rendered; a bountiful supper was furnished, and, after doing it ample justice, I was glad to crawl off to bed. The next day, a full account of the adventure, on my part, and a liberal collection on that of the guests, ended the matter for the present. I was so lame that I had to sit down all day, and was unable to work.

Third Summer

Ice Blockade on the Ammonoosuc

EARLY IN the spring, I was again called to return to the Profile House. Bitter experience, in former seasons, had taught me that I might expect snow-storms and wintry weather, and so I took the precaution to be provided for such contingencies. A thick riding-blanket and warm mittens are excellent companions on such a journey.

Arriving at Franconia by stage, from Littleton, I was not a little amazed to find solid cakes of ice, large and small, scattered all over the town, in the fields, gardens, and orchards, not omitting the open doors of barns and sheds. Some of the front doors of the dwellings were completely blocked up, and the whole appearance of things generally was most singular. It appeared as if the spirits of the Mountains had been having a grand *mêlée*, the weapons being cakes of ice. I am not sure which side beat. Upon inquiring into the cause of this strange appearance, I learned that a sudden freshet had taken place on the Ammonoosuc River, caused by the snow melting along the ravine of Mount Lafayette, and the water had rushed down, breaking the ice in the river into fragments, which were carried all over the town when an ice-jam occurred, which kept the water back, and submerged the town some three feet. This accounted for the ice in such unusual places. The road had been cleared out to make travelling possible.

While we were preparing to go forward, we were suddenly overtaken by a violent snow-storm, which came almost unheralded. We were prepared for it—our stout blankets keeping us comfortable—but the snow very soon became too deep for the stage to proceed on wheels, so we were obliged to halt, and hold a consultation.

We determined to go on, in spite of the storm, provided we could find some sort of a sled large enough to take us all along. There were about a dozen of us, all told, and not afraid of the weather. After considerable search, we procured a wood-sled belonging to a farmer near by; and having hitched our horses to it, and enveloped ourselves in our blankets and buffalo-robes, the driver cracked his whip, and off we started in high glee. The way was rather uncertain, but soon the storm ceased, almost as suddenly as it commenced, and we had a splendid moonlight ride through the gloomy forest, arriving safely at the Profile House. Here a rousing fire and a hot supper soon put us to rights, and the evening passed in great good humor. The next morning's sun revealed snow-drifts reaching twenty feet in height.

A Visit to the Other Side of "Cannon Mountain"

I started off, one day, with the intention of visiting the scene of the great conflagration caused by a fire kindled by some careless company of gentlemen, in the woods, years ago, on the other side of "Cannon Mountain." Ascending by the path which leads to its top, I soon reached it, and struck into the pathless woods, coming out, after a while, directly upon the place I sought. It was a desolate waste, of fifteen square miles; a wilderness of jagged and shattered rocks, charred stumps, and tangled briars, upon which the sun beat down in unobstructed fervor, making the place a very purgatory. The purgatorial appearance of the place was much increased by the presence of clouds of midgets (wood-flies), which pursued me with unrelenting vigor throughout my visit, obliging me to keep one hand continually in motion, to defend myself from their attacks. I had intended to explore the place sufficiently to obtain a fair idea of it, and then retrace my steps. I picked my way up and down, over and among the rocks, many of which were of immense size, and all looked as if rent and scattered by some great convulsion of nature, for angular shapes were universal; there not being a round, naturally-shaped rock within the range of my vision. Coming to a place where the rocks shot sheer down for several feet, I jumped off without due calculation, and the impetus of the leap carried me much farther than I had intended to go. When I finally brought up, I found myself in a sort of amphitheatre, the open side of it being directly ahead of me in the direction I had been pursuing, while above and behind me, the steep ascent forbade return. I had, therefore, to keep on, and trust to reaching the woods at the foot of the Mountain, through which I must find my way, in a roundabout direction, to the hotel.

The rocks around me abounded in remarkable resemblances to such things as tombs, pulpits, water-wheels, etc., and but a slight stretch of the imagination was necessary to conjure up many other things, even animals and persons, from the maze of fantastical shapes around. It was impossible to make haste, so I proceeded at a slow pace, stopping now and then to examine whatever attracted my attention; sending rocks down the steep places, to see them fly to splinters at the bottom, and otherwise amusing myself. I finally reached the woods, after a tiresome tramp, and, in their cool shade, I stopped to rest and eat my luncheon. Having duly refreshed myself, I took observations, and plunged into the woods in the direction of home. After getting several falls, tearing my clothes to tatters, and being several times at fault, I found myself in a familiar locality, and had no further trouble in getting home.

An Avalanche on "Bald Mountain"

In reviewing my visit to the desolate region referred to above, my rolling of rocks down the steeps, and the effects thereof, made me desirous of witnessing the same thing on a grander scale.

I remembered, in one of my visits to "Bald Mountain," so called from its lofty top being round and bare, to have seen an immense boulder of granite standing upright, quite near the brink of a long, steep incline which shot clear from the top of the Mountain to the line of forest, and far below it. I thought it would be fun to roll that boulder down the steep; but, how to do it? I paid two or three visits to the spot, to calculate the possibility of starting it, and to ascertain what implements were necessary, and how many hands would be required. Having completed my arrangements, I broached the subject to some of the workmen. It was a Saturday afternoon, and work was dull. The idea was readily taken up, and a party of seven men, besides myself, started for the top of the Mountain, distant about five miles. We carried wooden levers. Arriving at the spot, we arranged our implements, and applied them at the proper place, having first tried our united strength on it, and found it immovable. As the lever was steadily applied to the rock, it gradually yielded; and, as soon as its balance was sufficiently disturbed to insure its going over, a sharp, quick jerk was given to the bar, and we scattered instantly, turning, as soon as we reached a safe distance, to watch the effect. The rock turned over slowly once or twice, and then, gathering headway at each revolution, it thundered down the slope at a tearful rate of speed, raising great clouds of smoke and dust, and drawing streams of fire from the rocks over which it tore its way. We saw it reach the forest line, and we saw the tall trees go down before it like grass before the mower's scythe.

It disappeared from view, leaving a long, broad avenue behind it. That rock was the most speedy and effective path-maker that I ever saw. After all was over, I followed the trail of the rock down the slope, and was astonished at the ruin it had wrought. It was exactly as if a tornado had been along.

Retracing my steps, I joined the rest in a lunch; having finished it, we went leisurely back to the Profile House, well satisfied with the result of our afternoon's frolic.

Walker's Falls

These Falls, although well worth seeing, and comparatively easy of access with a competent guide, are yet neglected by the great majority of tourists. In fact, judged by the general practice of visitors, to have been *to* the Mountains is one thing, to have been over them—to have "done" them—is quite another.

I have already related how I went in search of the gentleman who got lost in the attempt to find these Falls without a guide, and the incidents connected therewith. The next spring I went with a gumming party to guide them to the Falls. The Mountains are covered mostly with spruce-trees, on which chewing-gum can be found in abundance, especially on the sunny side of the hills. Parties often go after gum. They carry poles about eight feet long, having chisels fastened to the smaller end, with which to cut off the gum when found high up the trees. The return of such a party, and the distribution of the gum, causes an amount of chewing that would astonish a cow. The distance from the Profile House was about five miles. There was enough snow still on the ground to render it difficult to find the true path, and leaves and dead branches had been strewed around so thickly the previous winter, as to increase the perplexity of a first passage, to the extent of making the way rather devious. I was several times at fault; and, most of the party getting tired out, voted to return, which they did, and got lost, caught in a heavy shower, and were thoroughly soaked long before they struck the road leading to the hotel. Two of the party pushed on, taking me with them; we soon found the path, and shortly arrived at the Falls, in viewing which we found ample satisfaction for coming. Sated with views of the rushing waters, and the surrounding scenery from various points, we finally turned into the woods in search of gum. One of us struck the fresh track of a deer, and, entirely forgetting the coming storm, which had been gradually darkening the air for some time, we gave chase, hoping to see the animal. We continued the pursuit until the heavy pattering of the rain brought us to our senses. Halting on the top of a slight elevation, we saw that we were completely lost. My two companions now wished that they had returned with the main body of the party, although, as it afterwards appeared, had they done so without me they would have been no better off. After some search, I saw a landmark which had a familiar look, and was sure that, by taking a downward direction, we should strike the bridle-path. The other two, however, insisted on going in the opposite direction, and I deferred to them so far as to let them try it, although I was morally certain that we should become still more involved in the mazes of the forest. They went up and down for two hours, without success, and then gave it up. By this time we were thoroughly wet and tired. Turning about, and bidding them follow, I sped down the side of the mountain as straight as possible, through mud, mire, and bushes, over rocks, stumps, and logs, dodging here and there to avoid the trees, and gaining impetus at every step, until we reached the low lands, where I looked about for a running stream, knowing that if I could find one I could easily tell, by the direction in which it ran, which way to go. Finding one, we followed it down, and soon came to a familiar path, which led us safely out of the difficulty. Had the two men been left to themselves, it would probably have been a "gone case" with them.

A few weeks after this I went out again, with the intention of examining the Falls, and more thoroughly exploring their neighborhood. I was advised not to go, as the weather threatened to be bad; but, even while admitting the fact, I went. I reached the foot of the Falls, and had commenced the ascent, when I discovered a violent thunder-storm approaching. There was a cave situated in the side of the cliff, which was called Lion's Cave, some eighty rods above my head, which promised shelter if I could reach it in season. I hastened up the steep ascent, much of the way on my hands and knees, until I had nearly reached it, when my progress was barred by a chasm, not visible from below. One side of the chasm was higher than the other; and, taking my hatchet from my belt, I felled and roughly trimmed a stout sapling, which I laid, across the chasm, and which, half-ladder, half-bridge, enabled me to cross and gain the coveted shelter. I had imagined it to be a huge cleft in the rock, but it proved to be only about six feet deep, and not high enough for me to stand up in, although I could sit comfortably, and be perfectly sheltered. The shower burst soon; the rain drove in sheets across the valley below me; it poured down from the Mountain above, forming a thick, unbroken curtain before the mouth of the cave; a miniature Niagara, in fact, which tossed and tumbled down the slope into the brook below, now swollen to a river. I enjoyed the scene vastly; but the omnipresent midgets soon found me out, and attacked me, seriously interfering with my pleasure, and forcing me to make a fire and smoke them out. In the course of an hour, the shower ceased as suddenly as it had begun. Descending from my elevated perch, and deferring my intended explorations to a future time, I went home, and was jeered and laughed at for my folly, until they discovered that my clothes were dry, when they stopped laughing, and desired particulars, which I gave them.

At another time, an old lady insisted on visiting the Falls, and engaged me as guide. In company with several men and two ladies, she hired a team, and set out. When the party reached the spot where persons wishing to visit the Falls must alight, and take the foot-path, all except the old lady had changed their minds, and decided to keep on and visit the Basin. She adhered to her original intention, and, after ordering the team to wait for her on its return, she jumped out, and I followed her, the rest of the party going on. Looking up, previous to entering the woods, I saw that one of the sudden storms peculiar to Mountain regions had stolen upon us unawares, was rearing its crest above the tree-tops, and would soon burst upon us. If those who had gone on should see the storm in season, they would return at full speed; but that would not save any of us from a drenching, and I determined to risk being left for the present, and shelter my companion. Calling her attention to the storm, she readily comprehended that we could not visit the Falls, and signified her willingness to go wherever I chose. I led her away some distance into the woods, to a broad, overhanging rock, which I had noticed in a previous ramble, underneath which I fixed seats for her and myself, and got snugly settled just as the shower came on. The thunder roared; the lightning flashed; the tall forest-trees bowed and writhed under the violence of the wind, and the rain fell in torrents; but we were safe and dry, and could calmly look out and enjoy the really sublime spectacle. The old lady was in high glee at the thought of the miserable plight in which the rest of the party must necessarily be, without protection of any kind. After the rain had passed away, she listened for the team, and when she heard it coming up the road, we proceeded to its side and waited for it to come up. It was a sorry-looking company that we beheld—all wet, draggled, and woe-begone; and we laughed heartily, both at their appearance and at their unfeigned astonishment at our dry and comfortable condition. We got in, and dashed away for the hotel, where our wet companions hurried off in search of dry clothing and fires. The old lady stood up all the way, declining to sit down where everything was soaked, and she chuckled right merrily, to think that insisting on going to the Falls had saved her from a wetting.

Fireworks on Profile Lake

It had become a regular custom for those guests who had passed the season at the Profile House, to get up some sort of a party or picnic before separating, as a fitting close for their holiday season. I almost always had a hand in the arrangements, for the hotel-keeper generally recommended me as a handy-man on such occasions. Being somewhat ready-witted, and withal not afraid of a little hard work, I usually managed to give satisfaction.

Once I had been requested to make preparations for a jolly good time at the old Flume House, which was then unoccupied. A party of about fifty ladies and gentlemen proposed to have a supper and ball, and I was somewhat nonplussed to arrange for their comfort, as there was no furniture in the building, and it was six miles distant from the Profile House. However, at it I went, cutting up fence-boards for tables, and made seats by the aid of work-benches. The dining-hall I decorated with evergreen as well as I could, and made it look quite respectable. Many delicacies had been sent all the way from New York, and the other viands were procured from the Profile House.

By dint of hard work, I managed to get all ready for company; and in the afternoon a long line of carriages appeared, with flags flying and music playing. The party was received with due ceremony, and ushered into the parlors, where they deposited their extra clothing. Then came a hop, and afterwards a large fire was built outside, where some green corn was roasted in a primitive manner. When all things were ready, the party was ushered into the dining-hall, and were much surprised at the appearance of the tables. Everyone seemed to enjoy the scene, and made the hall ring with their jokes and laughter. Then came toasts and speeches, the leader of the party occupying an old wagon-seat which I found in the barn. Their merry-making lasted until midnight, when all returned to the Profile House, highly gratified with their entertainment, and unanimously voting that the whole occasion was a decided success, even if it was improvised by a deaf-mute.

But there was another occasion which, while the management of it bothered my brains somewhat, yet proved to be a very agreeable and brilliant affair.

At a distance of about eighty rods from the hotel is a pretty sheet of water, called Profile Lake; or, more properly, "The Old Man's Washbowl." Surrounded by high hills and a dense forest, it has a most somber appearance, particularly at night. The idea was started by a gentleman from New York, connected with the *Journal of Commerce*, and another from Philadelphia, of having a row on the lake at night, with a grand display of fireworks. When asked if I understood how to manage the rockets, etc., I had to plead partial ignorance; but did not doubt that I could make a proper display with a little instruction. So the whole arrangement of the night's display was left to me, and a busy time I had of it for two days; the fireworks had been ordered from Boston, and arrived in due time. Procuring all the boats that could be found on Echo Lake and Profile Lake, eighteen in all, we had them cleaned, and fitted up with a Chinese lantern at each end. I went to the other end of the lake, about a quarter of a mile from the boat-house, and prepared a big pile of dry and green boughs, twigs and brush, all ready for a bonfire. Then I had a large ball, some two feet in diameter, made of rags, well smeared with tar, fastened to the top of a pole about twelve feet high, which I set on a float made from an old barn-door, and anchored it in the middle of the lake.

When the evening came, I was all ready for our grand celebration. Before the select party who were to occupy the boats arrived, with the assistance of one man, I had all the Chinese lanterns lighted up with sperm candles, presenting a very pretty spectacle. Then came the party down the road, headed by a band of music, and followed by nearly all the guests from the hotel who wished to witness the novel scene. Our brilliant fleet of boats was quickly filled by the ladies and gentlemen, with the band, while I had gone out into the lake in a boat, with one assistant to help me about the rockets, which I fired from time to time amid the cheers of the spectators. The effect was very brilliant, for the night was very dark, and no stars appeared to interfere with the general effect. The glare of the rockets and Roman candles presented a magnificent, yet peculiarly somber appearance, which quite astonished the spectators, who fairly yelled with delight. I could see by the light of the lanterns, that the party in the boats were quite excited, waving their handkerchiefs and huzzaing.

I now pushed off to the pile of brush and lighted it, and quickly rowed away, so that I might not be seen. It soon worked up into a strong blaze, causing the flames to ascend some forty feet; this had a novel effect, lighting up the whole lake. After this had subsided, I set fire to the grand illuminator on the float, which I did by means of a rag saturated with oil, at the end of a long stick; at the same time setting the raft to rocking, so that the pole appeared to wave to and fro, like a vessel on a high sea. The effect of this was very brilliant, also, and it burned quite a while. The performance closed with another display of fireworks, the various colors having a peculiarly beautiful effect with such weird surroundings. The party appeared to be satisfied with the entertainment, and rowing back to the boat-house, they landed, taking the Chinese lanterns for company, marched back to the hotel, enlivening the way with songs and cheers. On arriving at the hotel a sumptuous supper was in readiness, and a hop in the grand saloon closed the evening's amusement. I received many thanks for my part of the performance, and I look back with much pleasure upon that evening spent on Profile Lake.

One incident somewhat marred the enjoyment of one of the party—a lady, who disdained any assistance on leaving the boat. Being rather stout and solid, she contrived, while standing upon the edge of the boat and trying to spring upon the platform, to push the boat away from it, and her ladyship fell plump into the water. She was quickly rescued, but thoroughly soaked; and quite disgusted with the sudden change of scene. Hurrying to the hotel, she was quickly arrayed in dry clothing, and means to be a little more careful next time.

The next morning one of the guests, seeing the preparations for leaving by so many of his friends, concluded to attempt one more piece of fun; and so, before the stages were ready, he called me to his aid with half a dozen others of the employees. He rigged us up in grotesque costumes, consisting of the oldest and oddest garments that could be found. Guns, brooms, or wooden swords furnished our armament; and with huge pieces of tin upon our breasts, we presented an appearance much like Falstaff's brave army. Thus equipped as genuine country police, we waited in a side-room until the stages began to fill up, when we suddenly marched out, and going directly into the office of the hotel, pretended that there had been some pickpockets at work. We arrested several of the most prominent of the party, and took them into one of the public rooms, where we searched them, and made a pretense of finding the lost wallets. A mock trial was commenced at once; and it being soon discovered that it was all a sham, the evidence proceeded, to the great amusement of the bystanders. The jury finally acquitted the prisoners of any positive act of wrong-doing, and they were dismissed by the learned judge, with an injunction to be careful and never do so again, or the majesty of the law might visit them with some punishment awful to contemplate. This farce over, the departing guests gave us a round of cheers, and they rolled away to the duties and cares of life in the outside world.

After so much fun and amusement, I found it rather hard to settle down again to daily labor; but the summer was passing, and there was work to be done before cold weather should put an embargo on our labors. So I soon settled down to it, and gave my brains a resting-spell, while my hands and tools found plenty to do to keep off any sense of loneliness.

My Last Adventure, and a Trip around the Mountains

As COLD WEATHER was approaching, and the work so far completed to the satisfaction of the proprietor of the hotel, all the workmen were dismissed, and informed their services would not be required next year; so I concluded on bidding adieu to the Mountains.

I had calculated on making further explorations, in other inaccessible places, if I had time and opportunity, but finally gave up the idea, getting somewhat wearied of the "Adventures." I therefore turned my thoughts to Boston, as the most suitable field for me to labor in for the welfare of the Deaf-Mutes; but before taking my final leave, I decided on a trip around the White Mountains, intending to make the best use of my time.

Packing up my tools and trunk, I forwarded them home, not wishing to encumber myself with anything but a warm blanket. The prospect of a pleasant journey—one hundred and thirty miles—was very cheering, as the weather was unusually pleasant for the season of the year. Bidding adieu to all my friends at the hotel, I jumped on top of the stage-coach, not caring to ride inside; if I had done so, many beautiful views would have been lost sight of. My first stopping-place was at Bethlehem; I made my way to the Bethlehem Hotel, where I met an old friend, who had been famous among the mountain people for his daring adventures, far eclipsing my own. It was he who offered to bet a sum of money that he would wheel a bag of corn, on a wheelbarrow, to Plymouth, thirty miles up and down hills, on condition, if he should win, that the loser should pay the stake, and provide him with a situation in one of the hotels. He was successful in his undertaking, though it was a very arduous task, taking a day and a half to accomplish. He rested at the Profile House the night he performed his feat. The wheelbarrow he used was decorated and varnished, and hung up in a conspicuous place in the hotel, with his name inscribed on it, as a reward for his triumph.

The view, as seen from the Bethlehem Hotel, was very fine, and in the distance loomed up Mount Washington, the direction which I intended to take. Leaving Bethlehem, we were pleasantly jogging along when suddenly, almost, a heavy rain-storm set in. Two of the men who sat on top with me jumped off, and got inside the coach, which was already full, leaving me to keep company with the driver. I was not in the least discomfited, but wrapped myself up snugly in my blanket, and pulled down the rim of my hat, and in a few moments I was drenched through and through. Not having any change of clothing with me, I was in a sorry plight, but resolved to make the best of it. In a short time the storm abated, and the sun shone out beautifully, and by its heat I partially dried my clothes, and soon reached the White Mountain House, where half an hour was allowed for changing horses, which I availed myself of by getting thoroughly dry in the kitchen.

After a ride of thirty miles I reached the Crawford House, and was immediately recognized by several who knew me, and invited to stay there, free of all charge. Not having time to spare, I hastened back three miles to the depot of the railroad up Mount Washington, and had the satisfaction of examining the engine and track; but was sorely disappointed at not having a chance to ride up, though fully satisfied of the greatness of its undertaking. Early next morning, before the guests were up, I had some lunch ready; and, with my cane for a companion, determined to take a day's tramp, and visit the Elephant. The outline of the rock shows the head, ear, proboscis and mouth. The Silver Cascade is a beautiful fall; the Pulpit is a curious, towering rock, by the foot of the mountain; the Old Maid of the Mount, and the Young Man of the Mountain, the Infant and the Wiley House, so famous in history for the destruction of a whole family of seven by an avalanche of snow and rock, were examined minutely, affording me much pleasure.

The Old Maid and the Young Man disappointed me somewhat, for I had an idea their faces were as attractive as "The Old Man." The outlines were not half as good as my old *friend's*. The Devil's Den, the Apron, and other places of interest were visited. I was not in the least molested by the midgets, as they had nearly disappeared with the approach of cold weather. The Wiley House is a very interesting place to visit; it contains several articles which belonged to the ill-fated family before mentioned, such as a table, crockery-ware, boots, hats, guns, etc. In most of the rooms the names of visitors are written all over the walls. I inscribed my name high up on the wall, having the advantage, in height, over most of the guests. I visited the spot where the unfortunate family are buried, and the great rock that rolled down the mountain. It seems they had been deceived by the echoes of the rolling avalanche, and fled in the wrong direction; they would have been saved had they gone across the road, on the opposite side. Their house stood uninjured.

Having satisfied my curiosity, I made my way back to the Crawford House, a distance of six miles. The sun was setting, and a rain-storm approaching from behind the mountain. Being three miles from the hotel, or any house to shelter me, I did not like the idea of being drenched, as I was before, by the Rain Fiend, as I called it; and fortunately I discovered a projecting rock a few rods from where I stood, and fled to it, barely reaching it before the rain poured down in torrents. I chuckled over my luck, for I always considered myself a lucky fellow. The rain over, I was glad to come out with dry clothes. I soon reached the hotel, and ate a hearty supper, for I was "as hungry as a wolf."

The next morning I met a man of whom I had some knowledge, who had been guide and servant at the Profile House. He was poor when I first knew him, but now he wore gold and diamond rings, and was very fashionably dressed. He had just married a rich heiress, from New York. It seems he was acting as a guide up Mount Washington, and amongst the party was a lady on horseback, who, at first sight, became violently enamored of him. After some billing and cooing, they were married, and he now rides in a two-horse carriage. He was a lucky fellow, indeed, and I wished myself in his place; but, on second thought, I remembered I had a loving wife, which is far better than a rich heiress.

The ride up Mount Washington had been entirely stopped, on account of the great danger of being caught in frost-clouds, which sadly disappointed me, for I desired to see the Tip Top House, and all the surrounding hills, but especially the monument of Lizzie Bourne, in whose fate I felt a lively interest. She had gone up with her uncle, a doctor, late in the season, and late in the afternoon, without a guide, and contrary to the advice of their friends. They both got lost in their ascent, and wandered about till dark. She had gone out of the path, and wandered among the bushes and shrubs, until nearly all her clothes were torn off; and, unable to stand the cold, she fell down and died. The doctor was discovered, nearly frozen, keeping guard over her, and was rescued. She was greatly mourned, and her remains were sent home. A monument was erected to her memory by her friends, with rocks found on the spot where she died.

It had been my intention to cross the Mountain to the Glen House, but I was dissuaded from it, no guide being willing to risk going up with me. To think of further stay would prove of no advantage to me, so I decided to hurry home direct, instead of carrying out my plan, and was sadly disappointed. I bade good-by to the Crawford House, and took a stage direct to Centre Harbor. One little incident I witnessed, which I shall never forget: As we were riding down a hill, I noticed a beautiful girl sitting on a chair, a rod or more from a lonely dwelling-house by the road-side, holding a pan in her lap, and in it were some blackberries in boxes of white birch. She was waiting the approach of stages to sell berries to passengers, as had been her custom. The horses were a little unmanageable, and the driver tried to stop them, putting his foot on the brake to allow the passengers to dismount and purchase the berries; but the whiffle-tree behind the horses knocked her over, and spilled them all. I discovered she had but one leg. She was an exceedingly pretty girl, and her head was covered with a profusion of curls. Fortunately she was not hurt; but being unable to stand up, and overpowered with grief at the loss of her berries, it was truly pitiable to see her. All the passengers heartily sympathized with her; they jumped out, raised her up, and kissed her, lifting her on her chair. Her hands were soon well-filled with money, to compensate her for the fright and loss. She was as meek as she was beautiful. How she came to lose her leg, I never learnt.

Reaching the Centre House, and crossing Winnipiseogee Lake on the steamer *Lady of the Lake*, I took the cars and reached home, highly gratified with my THREE SUMMERS' ADVENTURES.

PART TWO

Mr. Swett and His Diorama

Address by Mr. Swett

[WE GAVE a notice in the last Annals, of the miniature Battle of Lexington, constructed by Mr. William B. Swett, a former pupil of the American Asylum. Mr. Swett came to Hartford, and exhibited his work to the pupils and teachers of the Asylum, on Christmas day, and at the same time delivered an *Address*, which he had previously committed to writing. We insert it here, not merely for the gratification of his friends and fellow mutes; the frank simplicity with which he has laid open his experience, gives it a peculiar interest for every reader.

Mr. Swett disposed of his work, while in Hartford, to Messrs. Goodwin & Co., proprietors of an attractive and popular show; which comprises a number of pieces of a similar description. He at the same time engaged his personal services in their employ, on terms advantageous to him.

Mr. Swett was born deaf of one ear, and perhaps partially with the other. He lost hearing entirely at ten years of age, by the measles and mumps. His mother, also a deaf-mute, is a sister of Mr. Thomas Brown, President of the New England Gallaudet Association of Deaf-Mutes, and he has several other deaf-mute relatives.

The intelligent readers of Mr. Swett's story, will be impressed with the importance of providing thorough instruction

---

Mr. Swett's address originally appeared in the *American Annals of the Deaf*, 1, no. 1 (January 1859).

in the elementary principles of mechanics for pupils of a natural bent and capacity like his.—Editor]

Ladies and Gentlemen, the Officers and Teachers and the Pupils of the American Asylum—

I CONFESS, I am totally incapable of saying what the expressions of my heart are while I stand before you. I must leave you to imagine one's feelings after a long absence, to find himself back again here on this place he has so often trod in his school days; everything is brought back to his mind, the school exercises, religious services, &c., &c. I can not but say, that I offer up my heartfelt gratitude to our Heavenly Father for his great kindness in keeping me alive, and in his kind care of my life's journeying, and at last bringing me safe to this place I so long desired to see, and to feel again all its blessings I bore when I was a schoolboy; for even now I retain all those boyish feelings, and I still yearn to become a pupil again and commence with the A, B, C. Oh! let me again be under the rule of the teachers; let me sit in the same room that I used to, and study my lessons again; let me sit at the same table and eat my meals, and let me again sit in this dear chapel, where I may drink much of that religious teaching again, which I so often attended in my school days. All would have been forever darkness with me, but for the kind care of Providence, by which this Institution sprung up as if by miracle, and thousands of minds were enlightened, and thousands know their God. Allow me to say, that I owe all the education I got, and all the success I met with since I left Hartford, to the beneficent Institution itself, and to your (the teachers') kind care and exertions and your teachings. I have now returned with pride, to show the fruits of it.

You now ask, when did it originate in my mind to make this diorama, the Battle of Lexington? I will now proceed to give you all the information I am capable of remembering.

Once on a time, I can not remember precisely, but should think it was about the middle of my term at school, the pupils and myself were invited to see the diorama of the Battle of Bunker Hill at the City Hall. Time never can erase it out of my mind, on seeing the first scene, how I was startled and enraptured, and would not turn away my eyes from the moving figures, and I wondered if they had souls, until the performance was through. When, on leaving the Hall, and while on our way back to the Asylum, Mr. Turner came up to where I was walking alone, separate from the boys; he put his hand on my arm, and I could see by moon-light, with a smile, and asked me how I liked the exhibition; and what answer I gave I do not remember, but I am sure I made some remark which appeared to please him, and ever after he said nothing about it, nor did I attempt to say about it to him again. I tried to forget the beautiful thing, but could not, and have spent many restless days and sleepless nights. I dreamed of it while in bed, amused my mind in various ways by day. I do not exactly remember what the nature of the show was. I feebly tried to find out. I found I was too young, and destitute of inventive genius, as I have now in my older age. I have often told the boys that when I am older, I meant to make a diorama, but all the answers they gave me were none of the pleasantest. They believed a deaf and dumb person would never be able to make one, nor succeed in taking an exhibition journey. I determined to surprise them some way, if there was any chance, which I happily had on a Christmas day. It had been customary with them to decorate their sitting room with evergreen, pictures, and any thing they could find at their wit's end, and for my part I was too lazy to do any thing, and at the same time, I unconsciously kicked up a quarrel with one of the boys, when I forgot I had a beam in my eye, for I accused him of his want of interest in helping the boys. It proved a good lesson to me, and I got worsted by him. As if by magic, I forgot the quarrel, ran to the city, got some colored papers, and by the assistance of an old pupil I succeeded to a charm in making and arranging soldiers; I borrowed war-horse with an officer on, I made a cannon, I set it on the west shelf in the sitting room. Christmas evening came. The teachers came, next the ladies and girls, and at the head was the venerable Mr. Weld, to enjoy the sight of the decoration the boys had made. I can never forget, Mr. Weld, with a look which appeared like surprise, walked quietly up to the shelf, while I stood near by with both of my hands in my pockets; he surveyed the work with his piercing eyes so natural with him, he turned round slowly full before me, and with his face lightened up with pleasure, asked me who made those pretty soldiers, &c., pointing at them with his straight fingers. I told him it was I. Some of the teachers followed him round, and at this instant I got myself out of their presence; my heart beat with delight at the success; I learned to think possibly I could succeed in any work if I should try. Though very trifling as you suppose, yet it led me deep into thought for many years, and here is the effect of this memorable event. I learned two words, patience and perseverance. When I lay hold of any thing, I go to work with a will and overcome all difficulties if I meet them. You are welcome to make good use of this example in your work, toward the pupils; they will follow your advice and my example to good effect during their lives after they leave the Institution.

You would ask, why was I willing to devote so much time on the Battle, when I ought to have attended to other things more necessary? If I am to say all the particulars which induced me to pursue the work, it would tire you to hear at present, but I will give you a few reasons and make the story short: I was born to be an inventor, or so I thought I was. I have been a great whittler, a curious and amusing business from the age 24 years old to my present age. You are welcome to laugh to your heart's content, but I turned it to good account. I loved all kind of machinery, and often felt gloomy and sick they were not of my own invention, nor could I invent any. I have studied natural philosophy, and many things, but I was not content with it. I wished I had been thrown into a good field, where I could make myself the most useful to my friends and the deaf-mutes in general. I wanted to have a good privilege to improve my mind with writing language, &c., &c. I thought by going on a journey with a show there may be a fine time to go to learning again and to great advantage, by conversing with persons, who have any interest with me. Very happily I had it to my heart's content, and hope I may continue to enjoy it a long time. I have been very fond of military music and seeing parade, ever since I was four years of age. I commenced to practice on the drum at five years old, with a tin pan and a stick. I thought to myself, before I lost my hearing, when I grow up to be a fine soldier, I will handle the musket, or brandish the sword, ride on a horse, a plume in the hat and epaulettes on my shoulder, &c., &c. Often I would get a long stick, tie a string on one end for a bridle, and vault on it with pride, and gallop away with a wooden sword to my side and a cock's feather in my hat; but I was checked in my youthful career by being deprived of my hearing, and to this day I have a longing to follow the army. I had a brother who went but never returned. He was wounded at the storming of the castle of Chepultepec, and died from a wound. I tried hard to get the consent of Gen. Pierce to accompany my brother to the war, but the laws of the United States forbid deaf-mutes enlisting for the army. At the age of twenty-five, I determined to settle down. I married and settled down in my native town. I worked diligently at my trade, and after eight years of experience, I found the competition in the carpenters' business so great, I being a mute, I found it hard work to support a family. I have been much hindered in all kinds of work by sickness, and the expense more than I could get by steady work, &c. I hoped, if

I could take a journey with the exhibition, I might be able to make myself and family independent and comfortable.

All the success I met with on this work, is owing much to my wife's encouragement and kind advice. She would lessen or drive away any gloomy thoughts that I was always apt to bear, and she would bear all the troubles with me with great patience, and I confess I have been more than once morose and cross to her in the day of trouble, but thank her for her kind look. When I succeeded, after a long time, in finding out a method I could work the figures, how her eyes brightened up! and she foresaw I might eventually succeed in the show business, and she often and alone of all my friends urged me along, showing pictures of future happiness and comfort to us all, put to silence so much malicious stories against us; God bless her, and let her be forever an ornament and a precious jewel to me, a brute of a man, and may she always by her kindness and gentleness, lead me along to prosperity.

Again you will ask, where I began to plan and work on this Battle. It was in Nashua, to which place I moved and got work in a door-factory. Not long after, one day, I went to work gloomily, for I had met with a disappointment. At last, a show-bill was handed to me, and on glancing at a word, I was thunderstruck to find that the very Battle of Bunker Hill I loved to think of and doted on, was to be exhibited on the following evening, at the City Hall. My apron was off instantly, for how could I hold myself at such unexpected news. I asked leave of absence, ran home, swallowed up my supper, for I could not eat it from great excitement, and before I knew where I was, I found myself the first at the Hall, begged admission; the proprietor kindly gave me a free pass. I must leave you to finish the story how I enjoyed it. I commenced right away the same evening. I did not sleep a wink until the morning sun admonished me to go to work at the shop. First, I set myself to learning to make figures with a knife, and then to study the history of the

Revolution. There was a gigantic obstacle to overcome. I was undismayed, but sometimes I gave the work up in despair, and would have destroyed my plan and some of the works I had begun, but for my wife; she prevented my rash act. I fixed on Lexington, because I know it was the *first* place where the first blood was shed during the Revolutionary War, that rendered this country forever free from the yoke of Great Britain, and that I hoped it would be more attractive and interesting than any thing that I knew of. Before I had proceeded far into the work, I was compelled to remove back to my native place, by ill health and other circumstances. I have done this work, generally in evenings, and every spare moment when I was not engaged, and sometimes I would work on one particular thing all night, for fear what I found out would slip out of my memory. It will not be necessary for me to say any more than that I at last succeeded, after six long years of fear and doubts.

It is well for me to say, that before I began on this work, I had invented several things, such as doctor's pocket scales, a key and lock, an artificial water-fall, and two others; but they proved nearly all failures, except the scales, which I would have entered in the Patent Office, but I had no means to pay for a *caveat*. I have been, and am now, trying on a perpetual rocking, though I hardly know if I can succeed. I have borne the laughs of my neighbors patiently, and now if I had failed to make my friends take notice of this last invention, I wonder if I could have borne the disappointment again, but thank God I triumphed. I felt very gloomy, and made up my mind I was the most unfortunate man in the world. But not so with my wife. I first performed to her and my brother alone, and then to a few friends, who were delighted to see it, and advised me to make it public. I followed their advice, advertised a grand show to come off on a certain evening. The effect of such announcement from a deaf-mute, among my friends, can better be imagined than described. The hall was full, and I need not say what they said of it; they assured me of a perfect success by cheerings. After the performance, I ran home, I capered for joy, my wife laughed, I caught her, hugged and kissed her, our old puss flew away, my children were astonished, and what more can I say now.

Here let me introduce this gentleman, Mr. James Winston, who deserves your esteem, and of all the deaf-mutes also, as a worthy and useful man. He came nine miles and volunteered to open the first exhibition. His kind offer I gladly accepted, and I can never have cause to be sorry I have allowed him to accompany me on my tour of exhibition. I hardly know on whom I can rely so well for honesty and interest in my behalf.

How I went to Lexington to make a survey, is too well known to you. I reached home at midnight with ears frozen; my wife was up waiting for me. She had kept up a roaring fire; how I devoured my supper you had better guess.

I came here with this Battle, for I have been very impatient to show it to my dear teachers, and the pupils, and hope it will be the means of producing a beneficial effect on their despairing minds. They will learn to struggle against obstacles, and go to work with a will. I must stop and thank you all for your kind attention and your presence. I must say, the whole work needs to be repainted and altered, and all the other fixings done up nicely. I am unable to do it at present, but I hope I may be able to, and hope you and all my friends will give me encouragement and assistance. I have a plan which I intend to accomplish at no distant day, to render the exhibition doubly interesting. When I take leave of you all, I pray you will remember me, and I will be thankful to you all my life.

PART THREE

Manual Alphabets and Their History, with Sketches, Illustrations, and Varieties

Manual
Alphabets

FROM AN acquaintance with the manual alphabets which are contained in this book [see pages 83, 84] much amusement and instruction may be derived. Their use, by hearing and speaking children, directs attention to the written form of words and greatly aids them in forming the habit of spelling correctly, which is of so much importance to them in after life.

Deaf-mutes, for whose benefit these alphabets were at first invented, frequently misplace words, and construct their written sentences in a very ungrammatical manner—their knowledge of the English language (confessedly one of the hardest to learn) being more or less limited by their misfortune and other circumstances—but they seldom *misspell* a word. This fact alone is ample proof that the use of the manual alphabet, by which, in the main, instruction is imparted to them, is a great help to correct spelling.

The use of the manual alphabet requires that each word used should be spelled out; and it will readily be seen that practising it is, in reality, practising spelling, and that those using it must necessarily become proportionately correct in that important branch of education. It is capable of many uses, and will be found, when acquired, as is easily done by any person of ordinary intelligence, to be one of the most convenient things, at certain times and in many places, that exist.

In this connection, a brief history of manual alphabets may not come amiss. We quote from a late writer on the subject—

The manual alphabet is by no means a modern invention. There were manual alphabets used in very early times, as early at least as the time of Solon, the Grecian law-giver, who flourished about 500 B.C.

Dr. Peet, of New York, supposes that when Solomon speaks of those persons who "speak with the feet and teach with the fingers" (Proverbs vi, 13), he alludes to some mode of furtive communication on forbidden subjects, resembling the early manual alphabets, used by children in schools to exchange words without being detected by the master.

The earliest alphabets we know of were founded on the ancient signs for numbers. The Greeks and Romans, at a very early day, had a regular and ingenious system of notation by means of positions of the hands and fingers.

Pliny speaks of an ancient statue of Janus, at Rome, the hands of which were sculptured in the positions representing the number 355, which was the number of days in the lunar year of Numa.

The Greeks and other Eastern nations used all the letters of their alphabet for the notation of numbers. Hence, as every letter denoted some number—A for 1, B for 2, etc.—it was very easy to reverse this, and make each sign for a number denote a letter.

The Romans had an alphabet, used for communications which those making them did not wish to be known to the by-standers, in which each letter was denoted by touching some part of the face or body, the name of which began with that letter, e.g., *aurem* (ear), *barba* (beard), *caput* (head), *dentes* (teeth), etc. These alphabets seem to have been generally known, at least to the learned and curious, from very early times, and it is remarkable that, so far as we know, no one ever

The Single-Handed Alphabet

thought of using them for the instruction of the deaf and dumb till the time of Ponce and Bonet, the early Spanish teachers, the former of whom died in 1584.

The manual alphabet which is now used in French and American schools (the one-handed) was brought from Spain to France, and from thence it reached America through Dr. Gallaudet and Laurent Clerc, portraits and sketches of whom will be found elsewhere.

The two-handed alphabet has been used in England for centuries, but the one-handed alphabet, owing to its obvious advantages, is gradually making its way there, although the former has the advantage of being very generally known in society.

Of the two alphabets, the one-handed is certainly the most graceful and convenient. In a multitude of cases, we may have one hand engaged, and of course it will be hardly possible to spell intelligibly, if at all, with both hands, for instance, in riding, or holding an umbrella, or in reading from a book or letter in one hand.

Yet the two-handed alphabet has some advantages. Its characters, bearing more obvious resemblance to the

The Double-Handed Alphabet

forms of letters, are more easily learned, and they are visible at a greater distance and with less light. Experience seems to prove, also, that it is less fatiguing to the muscles.

Either alphabet can be used in the dark, after a little practice. In the dark, the sense of feeling comes into play, as the one who is spoken to must *feel* of the speaker's hand or hands, thereby discerning, by the position of the fingers, what letters are made.

In point of rapidity, actual trial and numerous experiments have failed to place the advantage, definitely, on either side; but the impression is that the two-handed alphabet, presenting, as it were, letters in larger type, can be *read* faster than the other by one equally practiced with both.

A deaf-mute of nimble fingers and quick perception will spell out the Lord's Prayer by either alphabet in about half a minute, omitting no letter. Some can do it in less, but not so as to be legible to average eyes. This is from three to four times as fast as an expert penman can write the same prayer so as to be legible, though probably three or four times as slow as it can be read orally, by one expert in oral reading.

Neither alphabet will, except in very rare cases, where flexibility of finger and quickness of visual perception are extraordinary, enable a practised speller to communicate a speech, prayer, sermon, etc., *word for word*, to another, although the *substance* can readily be given: and the attention of many interested minds has long been directed to the discovery of some substitute by which this can be done. Several plans have been proposed, but none seem as yet to meet the case, some because they are too complicated, and others from their evident inconvenience; but, in this age of progress and invention, it is perfectly reasonable to suppose that a substitute will hereafter be devised which shall meet all reasonable requirements.

The true way to educate children is to combine instruction and amusement or interest. The manual alphabet is just such a combination.

Varieties of Language

SPEECH, DOUBTLESS, was the first form of language; reading and writing came long afterwards. Deaf-mutes, in all nations, were long regarded as inaccessible to language: that idea was long since exploded. "Necessity is the mother of invention," and the modes of expression are now almost as various as the thoughts to be expressed. There is written language, spoken language, the language of signs, and many others.

To understand fully the importance or value of anything it is only necessary to be without it for a time. Blessings almost invariably "brighten as they take their flight." The value of language would be unspeakably enhanced in our minds by a temporarily enforced silence—a prohibition of all expression of thought. There could be no books, no newspapers, no telegrams, no conversation. The world would be a vast cemetery; the universe would stand still: for language is its life, and to stop language is to stop all progress, of whatever name or nature. There are forms of language which can be addressed to each of, the five senses—sight, hearing, feeling, taste, and smell. *Audible* language is that which can be heard, as the human voice, the lowing of cattle, the bark of a dog, etc. *Visible* language is that addressed to the eye, as writing, print, signs, expressions, motions, etc. Under this head come all the works of Creation. *Tangible* language appeals to the sense of touch, as the conversation of deaf-mutes in the dark, by feeling the letters of the manual alphabet on each other's hands. Those who are blind, in addition to being deaf and dumb, are very expert in this mode of communication. Laura Bridgman is a prominent example of this. In connection with this subject, Dr. Thomas H. Gallaudet once asked the following question to an assembled company: Suppose two perfectly dark rooms, with a thick partition between them, having a very small hole in it, and an intelligent deaf-mute in each room: could the two deaf-mutes converse with each other? The conclusion of the company was that, as they could neither hear, see, nor feel, conversation was impossible; but Mr. Gallaudet demonstrated that a conversation might be carried on by means of an alphabet of *odors* or *smells,* which might be conveyed through the hole on bits of sponge fastened to small sticks, as, A (ammonia), B (bergamot), C (cinnamon), etc. There was no pretense of making a practical use of the idea, the intention being simply to show that it might be done. So with an alphabet of *taste,* as, A (apple), B (butter), C (cheese), etc., by which a conversation might be carried on for amusement or experiment. The great and universal law of compensation is well illustrated in all this. There is also an alphabet of *expressions of the face*—A (admiration), B (boldness), C (curiosity), etc.

The subject is inexhaustible; but the above instances will show how varied are the methods of communication possible, and their practice will serve to while away many a dull evening, furnishing amusement and instruction for young and old.

THE practice of the manual alphabet will greatly advance the education of children, whether hearing or deaf mute.

EVEN for those who hear, it is very convenient, for there are times when they wish to converse *silently.*

Thomas Hopkins Gallaudet

THIS GOOD MAN, whom every deaf-mute regards as a benefactor in no small degree, and whose name and memory are cherished by that unfortunate class all over the country, was born in Philadelphia, Pa., Dec. 10, 1787. His family early removed to Hartford, Conn., which city was ever after the residence of the son.

His attention was early called to the existence of a neglected and unfortunate class of people called deaf and dumb; his warmest sympathies were enlisted in their behalf, and he sailed for Europe in 1815 to qualify himself as a teacher of the deaf and dumb.

He made the acquaintance of the Abbé Sicard—one of the greatest benefactors of deaf-mutes—in London, and went to Paris with him and obtained a knowledge of the system there employed. Returning to America, he brought with him Laurent Clerc, a highly educated deaf-mute, of whom more is said elsewhere, and established the American Asylum for the Deaf and Dumb at Hartford. He was its principal until 1830, and then resigned, but always evinced a lively interest in its welfare to his death.

In 1850 the deaf-mutes of the country united in presenting Dr. Gallaudet and Mr. Clerc with a magnificent service of silver plate as a testimonial of appreciation; and in September of the ensuing year multitudes of the unfortunate, besides the deaf and dumb, were pained beyond expression to hear that their loved benefactor had passed away from earth.

In 1854 the deaf-mutes of the United States erected a handsome marble shaft to his memory, on the lawn in front of the American Asylum; but his most enduring monument is in the hearts of those whom he benefited during his life.

Dr. Gallaudet was, during the latter years of his life, intimately connected with the care of the insane, and his labors in that sphere were both enthusiastic and effective. The following lines, written for his funeral service, most clearly exemplify the character of the man.

> He dies: the earth becomes more dark
>   When such as he ascend to heaven,
> For where Death strikes a shining mark
>   Through bleeding hearts his shaft is driven.
> Alike the sounds of mourning come
>   From humble hut and lofty hall, —
> Wherever misery finds a home;
>   And all lament the friend of all.
>
> He dies; and still around his grave
>   The silent sons of sorrow bend,
> With tears for him they could not save, —
>   Their guide, their father, and their friend;
> And minds in ruin ask for him,
>   With wondering woe that he is gone;
> And cheeks are pale and eyes are dim
>   Among the outcast and forlorn.
>
> He lives, — for virtue cannot die:
>   The man departs, his deeds remain;
> They wipe the tear, they check the sigh,
>   They hush the sob of mortal pain.

Love lasts forever; age on age
The holy flame renews its glow,
While man's brief years of pilgrimage
End in the dust of death below.

SUCCESS in life is very apt to make us forget the time when we "wasn't much." It is just so with a frog on the jump: he can't remember when he was a tad-pole, but other folks can.

THE number of deaf-mutes in our population is increasing, and an acquaintance with the manual alphabet will enable others to converse with them without the trouble of writing.

"It is an entertainment and a novelty to children to find that they can produce language in a new form."

GOOD DEFINITIONS. Jean Massieu, a French deaf-mute, contemporary with Laurent Clerc, and, like the latter, a teacher in the Paris Institution, once gave the following definitions:

Sense is an idea-carrier; hearing is the auricular sight; gratitude is the memory of the heart; hope is the blossom of happiness; and eternity is a day without yesterday or tomorrow.

PUNCTUATION. This great and important auxiliary to correct writing is much ignored and little understood. One needs a *system* to go by. Perhaps the following rules, by an "ancient printer," may be of assistance to some. They are admirable for simplicity, to say the least.

"I set up (type) as long as I can hold my breath, then put in a comma; when I gape, I insert a semi-colon; when I sneeze, I put in a colon; and when I want to take another chew of tobacco, I insert a period."

Laurent Clerc

THIS COMPEER and associate of Dr. Thomas H. Gallaudet, to whom the latter owed much of his success in exciting an interest in the public mind in the education of the deaf and dumb, was born in La Balme, Canton of Cremieu, Department of Isere, France, December 26, 1785. At the age of twelve he entered the Institution for the Deaf and Dumb in Paris, then under the charge of the Abbé Sicard, and ultimately came to be one of the best teachers there. Dr. Gallaudet, being unable to remain in France so long as was desirable to obtain a thorough knowledge of the sign-language, selected Mr. Clerc to accompany him to America on his return, and finally induced him to do so.

Leaving home, country, and friends for the sake of the yet uneducated thousands of deaf and dumb in a strange land, Mr. Clerc devoted himself to their instruction for more than forty years, until age and infirmities forced him to relinquish his post, when he was granted a pension for the remainder of his days, by the Directors of the Institution whose cradle he had rocked and to those growth he had so largely contributed. Ten years after his retirement from active service, on the morning of July 18, 1869, in the eighty-fourth year of his age, Mr. Clerc followed his companion, Gallaudet, to the other world. Like the latter, he was missed and mourned, and the memory of the two is inseparable in the deaf-mute mind.

In 1874 a monument, consisting of a shaft and pedestal, surmounted by a bronze bust of Mr. Clerc, was erected opposite that commemorative of Dr. Gallaudet in front of the American Asylum at Hartford, on which occasion, as on the previous one, large numbers of mutes assembled from all parts of the country to do honor to his memory.

To the labors of Gallaudet and Clerc we know of no more expressive tribute than the following lines by Dr. Abraham Coles of New Jersey:

Not less their praise nor less their high reward,
Th' unequalled heroes of a task more hard,
Enthusiasts, who labored to bridge o'er
The gulf of silence, never passed before,
To reach the *solitaire*, who lived apart,
Cut off from commerce with the human heart,
To whom had been, all goings on below,
A ceremonious and unmeaning show;
Men met in council on occasions proud,
Nought but a mouthing and grimacing crowd;
And all the great transactions of the time,
An idle scene or puzzling pantomime.
Children of silence! deaf to every sound
That trembles in the atmosphere around,
Now far more happy, dancing ripples break
Upon the marge of that once stagnant lake,
Aye by fresh breezes over-swept, and stirred
With the vibrations of new thoughts conferred.
No more your minds are heathenish and dumb,
Now that the word of truth and grace has come.

A TRUE man never frets about his place in the world, but just slides into it by the gravitation of his nature, and swings there as easily as a star.

Institutions for the Deaf and Dumb

IN NEW ENGLAND there are the following institutions, the principals of which can be addressed by those interested in deaf-mute children of whom they may know, who stand in need of education, for full particulars.

Day School for Deaf-Mutes, No. 11 Pemberton Square, Boston, Mass.
Clarke Institution for Deaf-Mutes, Northampton, Mass.
American Asylum for the Deaf and Dumb, Hartford, Conn.
In New York City there are two; in Buffalo, N.Y., one; and one in Rome, N.Y.
Other States have nearly all one each, and there is a National College for Deaf-Mutes at Washington, D.C.

All these institutions are the progeny, properly speaking, of the American Asylum at Hartford, and the system pursued in them, with two or three exceptions, is mainly that originally brought over by Messrs. Gallaudet and Clerc, subject to such improvements as experience has suggested.

The number of deaf-mutes in the United States is estimated at between 15,000 and 20,000.